THE IDENTITY CRISIS

THE SOUL RENEWAL SERIES

The Soul Renewal Series

Beloved, I wish above all things that thou mayest prosper and be in health, even as thy soul prospereth.

3 JOHN 1:2, KJV

Book One: Identity Crisis

Book Two: Breaking Emotional Dependency

Book Three: Healing the Wounded Soul

Book Four: Freedom from Anxiety

Book Five: The Power of Forgiveness

Book Six: Learning to Trust Again

Book Seven: The Prosperous Soul

THE SOUL RENEWAL SERIES
BOOK ONE

THE IDENTITY CRISIS

Finding Yourself Before the World Defines You

✦

DR. TOYIN OGUNDIPE

Vidaliz Press

THE IDENTITY CRISIS

The Soul Renewal Series · Book One

Published by Vidaliz Press

The Identity Crisis is Book One of The Soul Renewal Series.

This book is intended for educational, informational, and personal-development purposes. It explores identity, emotional well-being, relationships, personal growth, and principles for inner renewal. It is not intended to diagnose, treat, cure, or prevent any mental health or medical condition, nor is it a substitute for professional medical, psychological, psychiatric, or therapeutic care.

Readers experiencing significant emotional distress, trauma-related difficulties, anxiety, depression, or other mental health concerns are encouraged to seek appropriate support from a qualified healthcare or mental health professional.

The stories, scenarios, and examples appearing throughout this book are used for teaching and illustration. Unless specifically identified otherwise, characters and circumstances may be fictional, composite, adapted, or intentionally altered to protect privacy and communicate broader principles. Any resemblance to specific persons or circumstances is coincidental unless expressly stated.

The principles presented in this book are informed by the author's Christian worldview and by timeless biblical wisdom concerning human worth, identity, relationships, forgiveness, renewal, and wholeness. The book is intentionally written in accessible language for readers from diverse backgrounds and is not intended to function as a theological textbook or devotional work.

Scripture quotations, where specifically identified, are credited to their respective Bible translations in accordance with applicable publisher requirements.

ISBN: 979-8-9965425-9-8

First Edition, 2026

Printed in the United States of America.

Vidaliz Press

Dedication

To everyone who has ever looked into the mirror and struggled to recognize the person looking back.

To those who became what others needed, carried names they never chose, measured themselves by what they achieved, and quietly wondered whether they would still matter if the performance stopped.

To those who have been defined by rejection, failure, success, appearance, relationships, family expectations, painful words, or things that happened long ago but somehow continued speaking.

This book is for you.

For the person beneath all the roles.

For the self that became hidden beneath survival.

For the voice that became quiet while everyone else's grew louder.

For the part of you that is ready to stop asking the world for permission to matter.

May these pages help you separate what happened to you from who you are, release identities that were never truly yours, and rediscover the worth that existed before anyone applauded, rejected, chose, overlooked, praised, or misunderstood you.

May you become whole enough to love without losing yourself, strong enough to face truth without shame, and secure enough to grow without rejecting the person you are today.

And may you discover that renewal is not about becoming someone else.

Sometimes it is simply about finally coming home to yourself.

Contents

A NOTE TO THE READER

Before We Begin

✦

THIS BOOK IS about finding yourself, though probably not in the way you are expecting.

You will not be encouraged to walk away from the people you love, dismiss where you came from, abandon your responsibilities, or decide that being healthy means needing nobody. You will not be told that every difficult relationship is toxic, that every painful memory is trauma, or that everyone who has disappointed you should be removed from your life.

Human beings were not built to live without connection. We need people. We need community. We need somewhere to belong. We also need work that matters, responsibility, something to aim at, and the chance to contribute something beyond ourselves.

The trouble does not start with any of that.

The trouble starts when the things that enrich our lives quietly become the things that decide our worth.

There is a difference, and the whole book lives inside it.

You can love your family deeply without letting your family determine your value.

You can pursue excellence without believing that failure makes you worthless.

You can enjoy success without needing it to prove that you matter.

You can belong somewhere without disappearing in order to stay accepted.

You can be corrected without being condemned.

You can be rejected without concluding that you are unlovable.

You can survive something painful without letting it become the permanent definition of your life.

And you can love another person completely without vanishing inside the relationship.

That is the kind of wholeness we are going after.

IDENTITY IS MORE THAN FEELING GOOD ABOUT YOURSELF

Identity is not positive thinking. It is not confidence, and it is not the same thing as self esteem.

It is the framework underneath everything, the thing you consult without noticing when life asks you the questions that actually matter.

Who am I?

What makes me valuable?

Where do I belong?

What happens to my sense of worth when I fail?

Who am I when the applause stops, or the relationship ends, or the job changes, or the children grow up and leave, or life simply does not turn out the way I expected?

Those questions are not philosophical. They are practical, and they arrive whether or not you have prepared for them, because life moves. Relationships change. Bodies change. Careers end. Money comes and goes. Children grow up. Reputations shift. Even the roles we have carried for thirty years eventually come to an end.

If your identity is fastened to something that can change, then every change takes a piece of you with it.

A steadier identity lets you go through change without losing yourself in it.

HOW IT HAPPENS

Almost nobody decides to lose themselves. It happens slowly, and it happens through ordinary learning.

We find out what earns approval and what draws criticism. We notice which parts of ourselves make other people comfortable. We learn when to speak and when silence keeps the peace. We remember what brought praise and what brought rejection. And we adjust.

Adjusting is not a fault. It is one of the ways people survive, mature, cooperate and belong.

But sometimes adjusting becomes erasing.

We get so good at becoming whatever the room requires that eventually a simple question becomes difficult to answer.

What do I actually think?

Not what my parents think. Not what my husband or wife thinks. Not what my friends expect, or my profession rewards, or my culture celebrates, or strangers on the internet approve of.

What do I believe? What matters to me? What kind of person am I becoming?

And the most uncomfortable one of all.

Do I recognize the person I have become?

YOUR STORY MATTERS, AND IT IS NOT FINISHED

Some readers will come to this book carrying a great deal.

Perhaps you were rejected, or betrayed, or steadily made smaller by somebody who should have been safe. Perhaps you grew up believing love had to be earned. Perhaps you learned to achieve because achievement got you noticed, or learned to be indispensable because being needed felt safer than being known. Perhaps nothing dramatic happened at all, and life simply changed, and the person you used to be no longer seems to be there.

What happened to you matters. It deserves to be looked at honestly rather than hurried past.

But something can be part of your story without becoming the definition of your life.

You may have failed without being a failure. You may have been rejected without being unlovable. You may have been left without being unworthy of staying for. You may have lost something precious without losing your ability to live well again.

Learning to tell those two things apart may be the single most valuable thing in these pages.

Where the Wisdom Comes From

The principles in this book are shaped by biblical wisdom, and I want to say so plainly at the start rather than have you discover it halfway through.

For thousands of years those writings have wrestled with exactly the questions this book asks. Worth. Shame. Belonging. Rejection. Suffering. Renewal. Forgiveness. What a human being is actually for. That thinking has shaped mine, and you will feel it throughout, whether or not I stop to point at it.

But this is not a devotional, and you do not need to share my faith to walk this road.

Where good research helps us understand people, we will use it. Where ordinary experience teaches something worth knowing, we will look at it. Where old wisdom illuminates something that is still true, we will take it seriously.

The aim is not to bring every reader to the same conclusion about faith. The aim is to pursue what is true, honestly, and to find principles that help human beings live whole.

This Is an Invitation, Not a Diagnosis

This book cannot tell you whether something is going on that needs a doctor. It is not therapy and it is not treatment, and it is not a substitute for either.

Some things need more than a book. Asking for that kind of help is not weakness. It is frequently the most sensible decision a person ever makes.

What these pages can offer is a structured chance to look clearly at your beliefs, your patterns, your relationships, and the things you say to yourself when nobody is listening.

Some of it will confirm what you already knew. Some of it will be uncomfortable. A few of the questions will need more than one sitting, and you should let them have it. The goal is not to finish quickly. The goal is to meet yourself honestly.

ONE REQUEST

As you read, resist the urge to read this book for somebody else.

It is remarkably easy to recognize other people's patterns. You will catch yourself thinking, *my husband needs to read this*, or *this is my mother exactly*, or *my friend does this constantly*.

Perhaps they do. For now, let them have their journey. This one belongs to you.

When a question makes you uncomfortable, stay with it a little longer than is comfortable. When you recognize something unhealthy, resist shame. When you find something that needs to change, choose responsibility instead of self condemnation.

And when you meet a version of yourself that only exists because it was once necessary, do not despise that person. Understand them. They were doing their best with what they had.

Then decide whether you still need to live that way.

You are allowed to outgrow patterns that once protected you. You are allowed to question labels you inherited. You are allowed to reconsider conclusions you reached in your worst season.

You are allowed to become more honest, more grounded, more secure, more whole.

Finding yourself is not about becoming self absorbed.

It is about becoming settled enough in who you are that you can love without disappearing, serve without being consumed, achieve without needing achievement, be corrected without collapsing, be rejected without losing your worth, and walk through change without losing yourself.

That is where we begin.

INTRODUCTION

The Question Underneath

✦

THE FORM TOOK her ninety seconds.

Name. Date of birth. Address. Occupation. Next of kin. Emergency contact. Allergies. Current medications. She had filled in a hundred forms like it over the years, for schools and banks and insurance companies, and her hand moved down the page without any real involvement from the rest of her.

She was fifty one. She was in a hospital gown, waiting for a procedure that was almost certainly nothing, and she was mildly irritated about the parking.

Later that afternoon, a chaplain doing his rounds sat down in the chair beside her bed and asked her a question that was meant to be small talk.

So tell me a bit about yourself.

And she started with her job.

He listened, and nodded, and then he asked it again, slightly differently.

No, I mean you. Not what you do. Who are you?

Not her name. Not her profession. Not whose wife, mother, daughter, or employee she was. Not what she owned, or had achieved, or what people said about her.

Just her.

She opened her mouth to answer and found nothing there.

She tried again. She said she was a mother of three. He waited. She said she had looked after her father before he died, and that people at work called her the reliable one, the one everyone went to. He waited.

Every sentence she offered was about somebody else.

She stopped talking. Then she laughed, because it was either that or the other thing, and said something she had not known she was about to say.

I don't actually know. Isn't that ridiculous, at my age.

It is not ridiculous. It is extremely common, and it is the reason for this book.

THE QUIET LOSS OF SELF

Losing yourself rarely happens all at once.

There is usually no crisis. No breakdown, no divorce, no public failure, no terrible diagnosis. It happens slowly, through a kind of learning nobody signs up for.

You find out what earns approval and what draws criticism. You discover that achievement brings praise, and that saying no disappoints people. You notice which parts of you are welcomed and which parts make others uncomfortable.

So you adjust. You become easier to accept. More dependable. Less demanding. More impressive.

And somewhere along the way, adaptation becomes identity.

You stop asking what you want, because you are used to considering everyone else first. You stop mentioning what hurts, because you have become the strong one. You keep achieving, because slowing down makes you feel strangely worthless. You say yes when something in you is saying no. You apologize for things you did not do.

None of this means the person you became is fake. You may genuinely be strong. You may truly enjoy helping people. You may be ambitious, or generous, or hardworking, and all of it real.

The question is not whether these qualities are real.

The question is whether they are expressions of who you are, or conditions you have come to believe you must meet in order to be worth something.

That difference is the whole of this book.

When Good Things Become Dangerous Places to Stand

There is nothing wrong with a career. Nothing wrong with marriage, or parenting, or education, or success, or being respected. These are good things, and this book will not ask you to want less of them.

The trouble starts when something good is handed a question it was never built to answer.

Am I valuable?

If your career answers that question, what happens when the career ends. If your marriage answers it, what happens when the relationship changes. If your children answer it, what happens the year they grow up and build lives of their own. If being needed answers it, what happens the day someone no longer needs you.

Anything that can change is a dangerous place to store your entire identity.

Because when that thing changes, and eventually most things do, you can feel as though you are disappearing along with it.

I am not saying every difficulty you face traces back to this. That would be too neat, and it would not be true. People struggle for all kinds of reasons, some of which have nothing to do with identity at all.

What I am saying is narrower, and I think it holds up. Your sense of who you are shapes how you interpret yourself, other people, your setbacks, and your place in the world. When that sense becomes unstable, a great many other things become unstable with it.

An identity crisis, as I mean it in this book, begins exactly there. Not in a diagnosis. In the quiet moment when the things that influence your life start to define your worth.

AN EXPERIENCE IS NOT A CONCLUSION

Sometimes identity is not built from success. It is built from pain.

A relationship ends, and somewhere inside you a sentence forms: *I wasn't enough.* Someone rejects you, and it becomes *I am unwanted.* You fail at something important, and it becomes *I am a failure.*

Notice what happened in each case. An event became a conclusion. And the conclusion, left alone long enough, became an identity.

This will come up again and again in the chapters ahead, because it may be the single most useful distinction in the whole book.

What happened to you and who you are are not the same thing.

Your experiences matter. Some of them changed the direction of your life. Some left wounds that still need real attention, and this book will be honest about which parts of that work belong to it and which parts belong further down the road. But an experience can be part of your story without being allowed to become your name.

The same is true in reverse. Perhaps what you are carrying is not something done to you, but something you did. A mistake. A choice that cost you. Identity renewal does not mean pretending that did not happen, or avoiding what it cost. It means learning that responsibility and condemnation are not the same thing.

A mistake should become a teacher before it becomes a name.

SOMEBODY ELSE'S MIDDLE

Modern life hands us endless ways to measure ourselves against people we will never meet. Somebody is richer, thinner, younger. Somebody's marriage looks easier. Somebody reached at thirty what you are still working toward at fifty. And because we now carry other people's lives in our pockets, the comparison follows us into the kitchen and the car and the last ten minutes before sleep.

But it is rarely a fair measurement, because we compare our private reality with someone else's public presentation. We compare our beginning with someone else's middle. Our ordinary Tuesday with their carefully chosen best afternoon.

Then we ask why our life does not look like that.

Slowly, the question can turn into something worse. *What is wrong with me?*

Often the honest answer is nothing. You have simply spent too long looking into the wrong mirror.

SO WHO ARE YOU

This book will not hand you a five minute test and announce the result. Identity runs deeper than personality, deeper than preference, and considerably deeper than whatever happens to be trending today.

We are going to look at where identity actually comes from. Family. Words. Culture. Comparison. Achievement. Rejection. The need to belong, and the different need to be needed. And we are going to look honestly at the identities people build in order to survive difficult years, because naming them well is most of the work.

Some of what we find will need to be kept. Some will need to be questioned. Some beliefs may have served you once and no longer do. Some labels may never have been true in the first place.

That is enough for one book, and we are not in a hurry to get through it.

THREE THINGS IN EVERY CHAPTER

You will meet the same three tools in every chapter that follows.

A **Soul Mirror** is a short, direct question meant to help you recognize yourself. When one of them lands, stop reading for a moment. The recognition is the point, not the number of pages you get through.

Timeless Wisdom is a single principle, stated plainly enough to carry with you after you close the book.

A **Renewal Practice** is something to actually do, usually with paper and fifteen minutes. These are where most of the real change happens. A reader who works through the practices and skims the chapters will get more out of this book than one who does the opposite, and I would rather you did the practices.

WHAT THIS BOOK CAN AND CANNOT DO

It cannot make you whole. That is not false modesty. It is the honest size of one short book.

Some of what you are carrying may need more than a chapter and a good question, and where that is true, I will say so plainly rather than pretend otherwise. This is the first book in a series for exactly that reason. What was done to you, learning to trust again, finding peace, and the long work of forgiveness all have their own place further ahead, and none of them can be rushed by trying to fit them here.

This book has one job, and it is enough of a job for now.

Not to make you whole. To give you ground to stand on.

By the end, I want you able to tell the difference between what happened to you and who you are. Between what you do and what you are worth. Between the voice that corrects you and the voice that condemns you.

NOT ABOUT BECOMING SELF CENTERED

There is a real danger in any conversation about finding yourself. It can quietly turn into a conversation about nothing but yourself. My happiness, my needs, my comfort, my truth, until the whole world shrinks down to one person standing in the middle of it.

That is not where this book is headed, and it is worth saying plainly before we go any further.

Healthy identity does not make you more selfish. Done honestly, it should make you more capable of real love, not less.

When you no longer need another person to prove that you matter, you can love them without needing to control them. When you no longer need applause to feel valuable, you can serve people without quietly angling for recognition. When someone else's success stops feeling like a threat to your own, you can celebrate them freely, without the smile costing you anything.

Wholeness is not isolation. It is learning to remain yourself while staying deeply connected to others, which is a considerably harder thing to do than either extreme on its own.

At the center of all this is an old idea, simple enough to state in one sentence. Human worth comes before human achievement. Before the title, the money, the applause, the relationship, the success, the failure, before anyone had decided whether you were impressive at all, your life already had value.

That idea runs against a great deal of what modern life quietly teaches. We tend to live as though worth has to be earned in installments. Successful enough. Attractive enough. Needed enough. Then, finally, secure. But worth that has to be constantly re-earned never actually settles, because there is always another comparison waiting, another goal, another person to keep up with.

So perhaps the better question is not what you must become before you matter.

It is what becomes possible once you stop living as though your worth is permanently on trial.

That is a very different way to live, and it is what the rest of this book is for.

BEFORE YOU TURN THE PAGE

Sometimes the person you are criticizing today was simply the person who learned how to survive yesterday.

Thank them for getting you here.

Then ask whether you still need their methods.

The woman in the hospital gown went home two days later. Nothing was wrong with her, medically. She thought about that question for eleven months before she did anything about it, and I mention that because if you have been carrying this quietly for a long time without acting on it, you are in ordinary company, and you are not late.

We will meet her again at the end of this book. By then the question will have changed.

For now, sit with the one that started everything.

Who am I, really?

That question is not the crisis.

It may be the beginning of your freedom.

CHAPTER ONE

Who Am I, Really?

✦

SHE HAD MOVED to a new city eight months earlier, and the neighbors had finally invited her to something.

It was a Saturday barbecue, four backyards down, and she stood near the drinks table holding a plastic cup of lemonade she did not particularly want, because holding something gives your hands a job while the rest of you works out what to say.

A woman she had met twice before, whose name she was already starting to forget, came and stood beside her and asked the question everyone asks at these things.

So tell me about yourself.

She was ready for this one. She had answered it a dozen times since the move.

Recently divorced. Two kids, eleven and thirteen. Works in accounting for a logistics company, has done for nine years. Renting on Marlowe Street until she decides whether to stay in the district for the school.

The woman nodded along, and then, not unkindly, said something that stopped the conversation for a second.

No, I mean, what are you like? What do you actually enjoy?

It was such a small question. It should not have been difficult. But she stood there with her lemonade going warm in her hand and found that she had nothing ready for it. Not a wrong answer. No answer at all. She could tell you her ex husband's shift pattern, her son's soccer schedule, the exact date her lease ended. She could not tell a near stranger at a barbecue what she liked.

She laughed it off, the way people do, and said something about not having much time for hobbies these days, and the conversation moved politely on to somebody's new fence.

But she thought about it for the rest of the weekend. Not the fence. The other thing.

What are you like?

She genuinely did not know.

This is where identity work has to start, and it is a strange place to start, because it does not begin with what is wrong with you. It begins with a gap most people never notice is there, because most of us are never actually asked the question. We are asked what we do. We are asked how work is going, how the kids are, whether we are still with so and so. Every single one of those questions can be answered without any real contact with the person answering them.

So we get very good at the answers, and very rusty at the question underneath them.

Try it yourself, right now, before reading any further. Not what you do for a living, not your relationship status, not your family. Just answer this. What are you like?

If you found that harder than you expected, you are in the right book.

What Do You Do, and Who Are You

There is nothing wrong with describing yourself by what you do. Most of the time it is the fastest, most useful answer available, and there is no shame in reaching for it. If a stranger on a plane asks what you do, they generally want a two sentence answer, not a meditation on the soul, and giving them one would be strange.

The trouble is not that we describe ourselves this way sometimes. The trouble is when it becomes the only way we have.

Try this small experiment. Picture yourself being introduced to a room of strangers by someone who has known you for twenty years. What would they say?

Now picture something harder. Take away everything they would say. No job title. No marital status. No mention of your children, your house, your car, your degree, or the thing you achieved that everyone brings up. Strip all of it away.

What is left to introduce?

For a great many people, the honest answer is: not much that they could put into words quickly. And that is worth sitting with, because it means something has happened over the years. Not something dramatic. Something quiet and gradual, the same way a path gets worn into grass simply because everyone keeps walking the same way.

We started answering the easy version of the question so often that we stopped practicing the hard one.

ROLES ARE REAL, BUT THEY ARE NOT YOU

I want to be careful here, because there is a version of this teaching that goes too far, and it does real damage.

It says that all roles are false, that being a mother or a manager or a caretaker is somehow a costume you have been tricked into wearing, and that the real work of finding yourself means shedding every responsibility you carry.

That is not what this chapter is saying, and it is not true.

You may genuinely be an excellent accountant. You may genuinely love being a mother, and be shaped for the better by it in ways that matter. Roles are not lies. A great deal of who you are has been formed through the roles you have carried, and formed well.

The problem is not that roles exist. The problem is when a role becomes the entire answer, so that if it were removed, nothing would be left standing.

Here is a way to test the difference. Ask yourself what would happen to your sense of worth if the role ended tomorrow. Not the role itself continuing in some diminished form, but actually ending.

The job gone. The relationship over. The children grown and living their own lives four states away.

If the honest answer is that you would feel a very serious loss but would still, underneath it, know who you were, that role has a healthy place in your life.

If the honest answer is that you are not sure anything would be left, that is not a character flaw. It is information. It tells you exactly where to start looking.

What Gets Exposed

This is not a hypothetical exercise for everyone. For some readers, it has already happened.

The job ended, through retirement or redundancy or a company that no longer exists, and a competent, capable person discovered that the job had been doing considerably more than paying the bills. It had been answering the question of who they were, five days a week, without either of them ever noticing the arrangement.

Or the last child left for college, and a house that had been full of urgent purpose for two decades went quiet, and a parent who had spent twenty years being extremely good at parenting sat down in that quiet and did not immediately know what came next, not practically, but personally. Who am I now that nobody in this house needs feeding tonight.

Or a diagnosis arrived, and a body that had always simply worked, that had never needed thinking about, suddenly needed thinking about constantly, and a person who had never once described themselves in terms of their health found the illness elbowing its way to the front of every introduction, whether they wanted it there or not.

None of these people did anything wrong. They lived ordinary, often admirable lives, fully engaged in real responsibilities. But because so much of their identity had been built on top of something that was always, eventually, going to change, the change did not simply take the role. It took a chunk of them along with it, and left them standing in the wreckage asking a question that felt entirely new, though it had actually been waiting the whole time.

Who am I, when I am not being useful to anyone?

KNOWING ABOUT YOURSELF IS NOT THE SAME AS KNOWING YOURSELF

Here is the distinction this whole chapter rests on, and it is worth reading twice.

You can know an enormous amount about yourself without knowing yourself.

You can know your job title, your income, your family history, your health conditions, your daily schedule, your strengths at work, your weaknesses in an argument, your favorite restaurant, and your opinion on nearly everything, and still, if asked the plain question, come up empty.

This is because most of what we know about ourselves is descriptive. It describes what we do, what we have, what happens to us, what people think of us. It is true, and it is also, in an important sense, external. It could be written on a form.

Knowing yourself is a different kind of knowledge. It is not what you do. It is what you value when nobody is checking. It is what actually brings you to life, as opposed to what merely occupies your time. It is what you would choose if every single expectation attached to you disappeared overnight and you had to build a Tuesday from nothing.

Most people have never had to answer that question, so most people have never really tried.

BEGINNING AGAIN

None of this means you have been living wrong. It does not mean the last twenty years were wasted, or that the roles you carried do not matter, or that you need to blow up your life to find out who you are underneath it.

It means there is a question that has been waiting, patiently, underneath all the good and necessary things you have been doing. And the rest of this book is, in one way or another, an attempt to help you finally sit down and answer it.

We start here, because you cannot separate what happened to you from who you are, and you cannot stop performing for approval, and you cannot learn to belong to yourself, until you have at least a rough answer to the most basic question there is.

Not what you do.

Not who needs you.

Just you.

✦

SOUL MIRROR

If everything you do for other people were taken away tomorrow, what would be left that you could still call yourself?

TIMELESS WISDOM

What you do can be taken from you. Who you are cannot. Most people spend their lives building on the first without ever locating the second.

RENEWAL PRACTICE: The Subtraction List

Write twenty sentences that begin with the words *I am.*

Do not think too hard about each one. Write quickly, the way answers arrive when nobody is grading you.

Now go back through the list and cross out every sentence that names a job, a relationship, an achievement, a possession, or something you do for somebody else.

Count what survives.

Most people find two or three sentences left standing. Some find none at all, and that is not a failure. It is simply an honest starting point, and an honest starting point is worth more than a comfortable one.

Keep the list. We will come back to it later in this book, and you may be surprised at how much longer it becomes.

CHAPTER TWO

The Self Beneath the Surface

✦

DANIEL WAS THE easiest person in the room, and everyone knew it.

At the office party, people drifted toward him without quite deciding to. He remembered names. He laughed at the right moments, and meant it. When a junior colleague's presentation went sideways halfway through, Daniel was the one who stepped in with a joke that took the pressure off the room instead of off himself, and the meeting recovered because of it.

Later that night, driving home, someone texted him a compliment about it. *You always know exactly what to say.* He looked at the message at a red light and felt, for about four seconds, genuinely good.

Then the four seconds passed, the way they always did, and a familiar thought slid in behind it.

If they actually knew how much I was calculating in there, would they still think that.

Nobody in that office would believe Daniel struggled with anything. Ask his friends whether he ever felt like a fraud, and most of them would laugh at the question. Daniel? Never.

But Daniel knew something they did not. He compared himself to other men his age more than he would ever admit. He took criticism harder than he let on, and spent longer recovering from it than anyone would guess from how quickly he smiled it off. He worked the extra hour most nights not because the job demanded it, but because finishing something gave him a few hours of relief from a question he could not quite name.

He was not lying to anyone. The confident man at the party was real. But so was the other one, sitting in the car at the red light, and the two of them had never really been introduced.

Two People, One Body

Most of us carry some version of this, and most of the time it is nothing to worry about.

There is the self other people meet. Composed, capable, doing what the room requires. And there is the self that exists underneath, the one having the actual thoughts, feeling the actual weather, when nobody is checking.

Some gap between these two is simply part of living with other people. You do not say everything you think in a meeting. You do not greet a grieving friend with whatever mood happened to catch you that morning. Managing the distance a little is not dishonesty. It is closer to consideration, and a world without any of it would be exhausting.

So this chapter is not asking whether you have a private self and a public one. Nearly everyone does. It is asking a quieter question.

Has the gap between them become something you manage every day, all day, in nearly every room? Or has it stayed the small, ordinary adjustment it started out as?

Privacy Is Not the Same as Hiding

It is worth being clear about this before going any further, because the distinction matters.

You do not owe every person full access to your inner life. Privacy is not deception. Boundaries are not dishonesty. Deciding what to share, when, and with whom, is simply wisdom, and this chapter is not asking you to hand every thought you have to whoever happens to be in the room.

The shift worth noticing is smaller and more specific. It is the moment privacy quietly turns into hiding, when certain parts of you feel like they must never be seen, because being seen would change how someone feels about you.

That is when a person stops simply living and starts managing an image instead. What should I say here. What should I leave out. Will they still respect me if they saw this part. It can become such a constant background process that a person forgets it is even running, the way you stop noticing a hum in a room after you have lived there long enough.

What Might Be Underneath, If You Let Yourself Wonder

Here is a question worth sitting with rather than answering quickly.

What would happen if the people closest to you knew you sometimes feel like you are performing. That you are tired of being the strong one. That you do not have nearly as much figured out as your calm face suggests.

Most people carry some version of that wondering, quietly, and most people also carry a fear underneath it. Not simply *what would they think*. Something closer to, *would I still be wanted if they saw this.*

That is not only a question about other people's opinions. It is a question about identity, because if you believe a part of you would make you unacceptable, you will organize a great deal of your life around making sure nobody finds it.

We will come back to this more than once later in the book. There is a whole chapter ahead for the person who cannot say they are tired, and another for the one who cannot say no. For now, simply notice whether any of this sounds familiar. Noticing is enough for today.

Two other versions of this are worth naming here, since nothing later in this book covers them directly.

The first is the person who has become known for lightness. The one who makes the room laugh, who lifts a mood the moment it starts to sink, who somehow always has the right joke at the right time. This can be a genuine gift, and often is. But sometimes humor is doing quiet double duty, keeping a conversation moving fast enough that nobody gets the chance to ask a harder question. If the room is laughing, nobody notices you're tired. If you're the funny one, nobody thinks to check whether you're actually all right. The joke is often completely real. It can still be standing guard over something that never gets discussed.

The second is the person who has learned to want nothing out loud. *I don't really care either way. It doesn't bother me. I never get too attached.* Sometimes that is simple, healthy detachment. Often it is something else, a way of making sure that if the thing you actually wanted falls through, nobody, including you, ever has to watch you lose it, because officially you never wanted it in the first place. Caring is what makes rejection and disappointment possible. Announcing that you don't care is one of the more effective ways of trying to opt out of both, and it works, at a cost most people only add up much later.

WHERE THIS STARTS

Nobody decides, as a child, to build a public self. It happens the way most patterns happen, through small repeated experiments that eventually stop feeling like experiments at all.

A child cries and is told to stop crying. Asks a hard question and is told not to talk back. Gets excited and is told to calm down, you're too much. None of this usually comes from cruelty. Parents get tired. Adults make mistakes. Sometimes real correction is needed.

But repetition teaches something beyond the moment itself. A child can begin to conclude, without ever putting it into words, that certain parts of them make people uncomfortable. So the child adjusts. Gets quieter, or funnier, or unusually obedient, or endlessly capable, whatever seems to keep the room calm.

By adulthood, the adjustment rarely feels like a performance anymore. It feels like personality. In many ways it has become part of one. The question worth asking is not whether the adjustment was wrong. It often kept you safe when safety was not guaranteed. The question is only whether it is still needed now, in a life that may no longer require it.

You do not have to be harsh with your younger self to ask that question honestly. You can look back and say, I understand exactly why you became this. And still add, gently, we may not have to stay here.

WHAT IT COSTS A RELATIONSHIP

Daniel's wife knew about the car, in the sense that she had learned, over the years, not to fully trust how quickly he bounced back from things. She had married the version of him that occasionally sat in silence a beat too long before answering a question, unsure of himself in ways the office never saw. She loved that version specifically. But most weeks, the version of him she actually lived beside was the one who had already recovered by the time he walked through the door, because the recovery had become automatic, and did not require an office party to trigger it anymore.

This is one of the quieter costs of a managed self, and it rarely announces itself, because nothing about it looks like betrayal. Nobody is lying. Nobody is unfaithful. The person is present, functional, even warm. But a spouse can find themselves living alongside the composed version far more often than the real one, and can feel a loneliness that is difficult to explain, even to themselves, because on paper there is nothing wrong.

Two managed people, however affectionate, however committed, will settle at exactly the depth of honesty they have each been willing to risk, and not one inch past it. If you want to be truly known by the person you have chosen, they may need to meet you at the red light sometimes, not only after you have arrived home and rearranged your face.

WHAT WAS NEVER MEANT TO BE A SECRET

There is an old idea, worth holding lightly rather than preaching, that most people judge by what they can see, while something deeper pays attention to the heart. It is less a rule about other people and more a quiet observation about how we are known. The people around us, even the ones who love us, are mostly working from what we let them see. If the deeper self never gets shown, it can go years without being met by anyone at all, not because people do not care, but because nobody can love what they have never been allowed to find.

LETTING SOMEONE IN

None of this means abandoning your public self. You still need it. There will always be rooms that call for composure rather than raw honesty, and that is not hypocrisy. It is simply how living with other people works.

What might actually help is smaller than a total transformation. It is choosing one or two people, carefully, and letting them see the version of you that exists before you arrange your face. Not everyone. Not the whole office, or the whole family, or every friend in the group chat. One or two, chosen on purpose, shown more than once.

Choose them by what they have already shown you, not by how close you happen to feel to them today. A safe person can hear something difficult without immediately needing to fix it or judge it. They can disagree with you without humiliating you, and keep what you have told them exactly where you left it. If you cannot think of anyone who fits that description yet, that is worth knowing plainly rather than glossing over, and it does not mean you are meant to stay hidden. It means the work starts one step earlier than you expected.

This will likely feel uncomfortable, because the hidden parts of you were usually hidden for a reason, even if the reason was decided years ago and quietly forgotten since. Showing them again risks the very response that first taught you to hide. But staying fully composed for the rest of your life carries its own cost, paid slowly, mostly in private, mostly noticed only by you.

What might it be like, just for one conversation with one person you trust, to let the version from the car do the talking?

✦

SOUL MIRROR

What is the thing you are most afraid people would think of you differently if they knew it?

TIMELESS WISDOM

People fall in love with, and befriend, and hire the self you present. Only a few will ever be shown the self underneath. Choose carefully who gets to meet both.

RENEWAL PRACTICE: The Versions of Me

Take a page and write five headings: *Me at work. Me with family. Me with friends. Me in my closest relationship. Me when I am completely alone.*

Under each one, write a few honest words describing the version of yourself that usually shows up there. Do not overthink it. Confident, quiet, careful, funny, tired, defensive, whatever comes first.

Look across what you wrote. Which qualities appear almost everywhere? Those likely reflect something real in your character. Which ones change the most from column to column? Ask yourself, gently, why you believe that particular room needs a different version of you.

Then finish these three sentences.

People usually see me as ______.

What they often do not see is ______.

Something I would like to become more honest about is ______.

You do not have to show this page to anyone. It is between you and yourself, and for today, that is enough.

CHAPTER THREE

How Identity Is Formed

✦

THE DRAWING WAS of a horse, mostly recognizable, colored carefully outside the lines by a seven year old who had spent forty minutes on it.

She ran into the kitchen holding it out in both hands. Her mother was on the phone, balancing a pan on the stove with her shoulder, and looked down for exactly one second.

Not now, sweetheart.

It was nothing. Any parent would have done the same, on that particular afternoon, with that particular phone call. The girl put the drawing on the counter and went back to her room, and neither of them remembered it by dinner.

Except it was not really the drawing, and it was not really that afternoon. It was the fortieth time, or the hundredth, that a small offering had been met with *not now,* and somewhere in there, without anyone deciding it on purpose, a lesson had quietly finished installing itself. Years later, an adult who could not fully explain why sat in meetings with a good idea and said nothing, or was asked what she thought and answered, honestly as far as she knew, *I don't know.*

She may have known. She had simply learned, a long time ago, that what she thought was not the kind of thing people had time for.

LONG BEFORE YOU HAD THE WORDS

You were learning who you were long before you had any of the vocabulary for it. Before you understood words like identity or self worth, you were already receiving information about yourself, and most of that information arrived without a single word attached. A smile told you something. So did silence. The way a room responded when you cried taught you something about your own feelings, long before anyone explained what feelings were.

Nobody sat you down and announced that your identity was now being constructed. It happened around dinner tables and on playgrounds and inside ordinary Tuesday afternoons, through thousands of small moments you no longer remember individually, though you still carry what they added up to.

You did not choose most of the materials. But you are allowed, now, as an adult, to go back and examine what got built.

THE FIRST MIRROR

For nearly everyone, the earliest mirror was another human face.

A baby does not arrive already knowing whether the world is safe. The baby learns it, the same way you learn a language, by exposure and repetition rather than instruction. Someone responds to the cry, or does not. Someone returns, or does not. Long before a child can put a single sentence together, a set of quiet conclusions is already forming. Is this a place where I am wanted. Does my presence bring anyone delight. Can I trust someone to come back.

This does not mean one hard afternoon determines a life. Parents are human, and they get tired and lose patience and misunderstand, the way the mother in the kitchen did, without malice, without even noticing. What shapes a child is rarely a single moment. It is the pattern the moments make together, especially when they come from people whose love matters most.

Children Are Honest Witnesses and Bad Interpreters

Children notice everything and explain almost none of it correctly, and this matters more than it sounds like it should.

A child cannot understand exhaustion, or depression, or a marriage under strain, so when a parent goes quiet or distant, the child reaches for the only explanation small enough to hold. *It must be me.* A father leaves, and a child who cannot possibly grasp the adult reasons concludes, privately, that better behavior might have kept him. A home is short on money, and a child decides, without anyone teaching it directly, that needing things from other people is dangerous.

None of these conclusions have to be true to start shaping a life. A child does not require accuracy before believing something. Only repetition.

What Happened and What You Decided It Meant

Here is one of the most important ideas in this entire book, and it is worth reading slowly.

An experience and the meaning you assign to that experience are not the same thing, even though they feel identical at the time.

Say you were not chosen for a team. The event is simply that you were not chosen. But the meaning could be *I need more practice,* or *that was not my sport,* or it could just as easily become *I am not good enough,* and both meanings are built on the exact same afternoon.

Say a relationship ends. The event is that someone left. The meaning might become *we wanted different things,* or it might harden into *nobody stays,* or *I am impossible to love.* The pain is real either way. The meaning is not automatically supplied by the event. You participate in writing it, usually without noticing you are doing it, and whatever meaning you repeat often enough eventually stops feeling like an interpretation and starts feeling like a fact.

NOT EVERYTHING CAME FROM OUTSIDE YOU

It would be too simple to say everything about you was placed there by other people, so it is worth saying plainly that some of it was already yours on arrival.

Some children are naturally cautious. Others walk toward anything new. Some feel everything intensely and take a long time to recover. Others move on quickly. None of this was assigned by a parent or a teacher. It came with you, and it shaped how the same environment landed differently on you than it would have on someone else. A sensitive child can carry an offhand comment for years. A more easygoing sibling, raised in the very same house, might forget the same comment by dinner.

This is worth remembering whenever the explanation for your life starts sounding too simple, whether the sentence is *my parents caused everything about me,* or its opposite, *none of it affected me at all.* Identity forms in the space between what you brought into the world and what the world did with it, and both halves matter.

THE WORLD WIDENS

Family is the first classroom, but it is far from the only one.

Culture hands you a script early, about what success looks like, what a respectable life includes, how a man or a woman is expected to behave, and you absorb most of it before you are old enough to question any of it. We will spend a full chapter later in this book looking closely at that script and asking which parts of it are actually yours. For now, simply notice that it exists.

School does something similar, only faster and more publicly. Suddenly there are grades, and teams that pick some children first, and bodies developing at different speeds in front of everyone. A child who already privately wonders whether they are enough can experience one ordinary rejection as proof, while a child without that private wondering shrugs the same moment off by lunchtime. Small events start connecting to other small events, and eventually the connections become a story you carry without remembering it was ever assembled.

Families also tend to hand out roles almost without noticing they are doing it. The responsible one. The funny one. The one everyone worries about. That is worth a chapter of its own, and it gets one immediately after this, because a role assigned to you at eight years old has a way of outliving the child who first wore it.

Some children, meanwhile, learn a role by absorbing the room rather than being assigned it. One learns that being easy and needing nothing keeps the peace, and grows into an adult who cannot say the word tired. Another learns that achievement is what earns attention, and grows into an adult who cannot rest without guilt. A third learns that the safest place in a loud house is silence, and grows into an adult with excellent ideas nobody in the meeting ever hears. Each of those has an entire chapter waiting for it later in this book, because each one deserves more than a paragraph. For now, simply ask whether any of them sound like you.

Why Some Beliefs Feel So True

Some beliefs about yourself feel true because they are. Others feel true only because they are familiar, and it is worth learning to tell the two apart.

Think of a path worn into grass. Nobody engineered it. It simply formed because the same feet crossed the same ground enough times that the ground gave way and made the walking easier. Thought works in a similar fashion. A sentence you have repeated to yourself for twenty years, *I am not enough,* stops feeling like an opinion you once formed and starts feeling like solid geography, simply because you have walked it so many times.

That does not mean you are stuck there permanently. It means changing it takes more than one encouraging sentence. It takes noticing the old path is there, questioning honestly where it actually leads, and walking a different one often enough that it, too, becomes easy underfoot.

An Accurate Mirror, and a Distorted One

You have already met the phrase Soul Mirror at the end of the last two chapters, and here is where the name earns its meaning.

A mirror reflects something back to you, but not every mirror reflects it accurately. Stand in front of a warped one and the shape looking back is still you, only stretched and wrong. If it were the only mirror you had ever seen, you might believe the distortion was simply what you looked like.

The same thing happens emotionally. Someone treats you as though you do not matter, and their treatment becomes a mirror. A parent calls you difficult often enough, and the label becomes a mirror. But another person's treatment of you is not automatic proof of who you are. Sometimes it is a far more accurate reflection of their own fear, or exhaustion, or limitations, than it ever was of you. This does not mean every hard word should be waved away. Some mirrors are showing you something true that is worth seeing. The skill worth building is asking, each time, whether this particular reflection is accurate before you decide to believe it.

Understanding Is Not the Same as Blame

Some readers will notice, somewhere in this chapter, a parent's or a teacher's or a former partner's face coming to mind. That is a natural response, and it does not need to be resisted.

But there is a real difference between blame and understanding, and the difference matters for where you go next. Blame says, you made me this way, so my life is now your responsibility. Understanding says something quieter. This shaped me. Now that I can see it clearly, I get to decide what to do with it.

You can recognize that your parents made real mistakes while also remembering that they were very likely parenting out of whatever they themselves had been handed. They did not arrive in adulthood empty. A father who never once said the words I love you may have grown up in a home where love was shown entirely through providing, never through saying. A mother who worried about everything may have grown up somewhere genuinely unstable. None of this erases what it cost you. It simply widens the picture enough that you are not left choosing between two exhausting extremes, my parents were perfect, or my parents ruined everything. Almost nobody's story is that simple.

What You Can Do With What You Now See

Childhood handed you a set of conclusions. Adulthood hands you something childhood never could, the chance to actually look at them.

If somewhere along the way you learned that needing help was a weakness, you are now old enough to ask where that idea came from, and whether it has actually served you, or simply cost you. If you learned that your worth depended on succeeding, you can ask, gently, who you would still be on the day you failed. This book will come back to that exact process later, with a fuller set of questions built for exactly this purpose. For now, it is enough to know the door exists and that you are allowed to open it.

Not everything you were taught needs to be discarded. Some of it was wisdom, and worth keeping exactly as it is. But not everything you were taught needs to stay either, and telling the two apart is some of the most important work this book can offer you.

You Are Still Being Formed

Identity does not finish forming in childhood, whatever it might feel like some mornings. You are still changing. Marriage changes you. Loss changes you. A late diagnosis, an unexpected friendship, a failure you did not see coming, all of it keeps shaping the same ongoing project.

There is an old idea, found in wisdom far older than any of us, that a person can be renewed from the inside, that the way we think is not fixed forever simply because it has been true for a long time. That idea matters here, because understanding how you became who you are would be a fairly bleak exercise if nothing about it could ever change. But it can. You may not have chosen the first messages you received about yourself. You get to choose, starting now, which of them you keep carrying.

✦

SOUL MIRROR

Think of one painful thing that happened when you were young. What did you decide it meant about you at the time, and do you still believe it now?

TIMELESS WISDOM

You did not choose everything that shaped you. But understanding what shaped you gives you far greater freedom to choose what continues shaping you from here.

RENEWAL PRACTICE: The Three Columns

Take a page and draw two lines down it, making three columns.

In the first, write one experience that affected you. Keep it simple and factual. *My father rarely praised me.*

In the second, write what you came to believe because of it. *I am difficult to please. I have to achieve more before anyone notices me.*

In the third, write what else could be true. Not a forced positive spin, simply another honest possibility. *His trouble showing affection may have had far more to do with him than with my worth.*

Try this with two or three different experiences. The goal is not to rewrite your history into something more pleasant than it was. It is only to separate what happened from everything you quietly decided it meant, because that small gap, once you can see it clearly, is often enough room for an entirely different future.

CHAPTER FOUR

The Identity You Inherited

✦

AT THANKSGIVING, SOMEONE hands him the knife.

You do it, you're the responsible one.

It is said lightly, the way these things always are, over the noise of a football game and three conversations happening at once. He takes the knife and carves the turkey, the way he has done every year since he was old enough to be trusted with it, and nobody in that kitchen remembers exactly when the job became his. He does. He was seven, his father had just left, and somebody needed to be the one who did not fall apart. He was the oldest child in the room that could still be counted on, so he became the one who could be counted on, and thirty five years later, at a table full of people who love him, he is still the one holding the knife.

Nobody assigned him that role on purpose. It simply found him, the way roles usually do, in a moment that needed filling, and it has been his ever since.

GIVEN BEFORE WE HAD ANY SAY

Some things arrive before you have a vote. Your name. Your family. Your place among your siblings. The stories that were already being told about you before you were old enough to correct any of them.

Some of what you inherited is genuinely good. It gave you structure, or connected you to people and a history worth having. But some of it grew heavy without anyone intending it to, and some messages were repeated so often that everyone stopped noticing they were messages at all. They simply became normal. And what feels normal is not automatically what is healthy.

EVERY FAMILY TELLS ITSELF A STORY

Families carry stories the way they carry last names, some spoken constantly and some never said aloud at all. Stories about what makes the family proud, what brings shame, what a person in this family is simply supposed to be.

People in this family work hard. We do not depend on anyone. Family always comes first. Failure is not an option.

Some of that is wisdom. Some of it is fear wearing wisdom's clothes, and sometimes a single sentence is carrying both at once. Family comes first can teach real loyalty, and it can also mean nobody in the house is allowed a boundary. Be strong can build real courage, and it can also raise a person who has never once learned how to ask for help.

The useful question is rarely whether the message was good or bad. It is what the message taught you about who you were required to become.

THE ROLE THAT FOUND YOU

Almost nobody selects their first family role. It finds them, usually in a moment exactly like the one at that Thanksgiving table, a gap that needed filling and a child standing close enough to fill it.

Then something strange happens. The season that created the role ends, but the role does not. The child who became responsible grows up and becomes the adult everyone still calls first. The one who kept the peace as a kid is still smoothing over conflicts that were never really theirs to fix. Nobody renews the assignment. Nobody ever really asks whether it still fits. It simply continues, quietly, for decades, the way his did with a carving knife.

THE DANGER OF BEING KNOWN TOO EARLY

Families have a way of deciding who we are before we have finished becoming it. *This one is stubborn. This one is the smart one. This one is always trouble.*

The description often starts with something true. But repeated long enough, a description turns into a box, and every new piece of behavior gets read through the old label whether it still applies or not. The once unreliable child becomes entirely dependable, and the family still jokes about how you can never count on him. The shy child grows into a genuinely confident adult, and people at the table still speak for her out of old habit. Relatives keep meeting a version of you that stopped existing years ago, and because family voices carry real weight, you can find yourself quietly agreeing with them, even when you know better.

WHEN EXPECTATION BECOMES A TEST OF LOYALTY

Expectation is not automatically a burden. A parent who believes in you and pushes you toward your potential is often giving you something valuable.

It becomes something else when love starts to feel conditional on meeting it. Picture a family that has always assumed a particular path, law, medicine, the family business, ministry. If that path genuinely fits you, there may be no conflict at all. But if it does not, the choice stops being a career decision and becomes something much larger. Will I disappoint them. Will they think I wasted what I was given. Will I still belong here if I choose something else.

At that point the real question a person is answering is no longer *what should I do.* It has quietly become *who am I allowed to be,* and people can spend years inside a life they did not choose because changing direction feels less like a decision and more like a betrayal.

When Love and Approval Get Confused

Children notice approval before they can name the difference between it and love, and they will use whatever pattern is available to explain the difference to themselves.

If warmth mainly shows up around success, a child may quietly conclude that success is what earns love. If affection cools during disagreement, the lesson becomes that agreement is what keeps it safe. Nobody has to say any of this directly. Children build the meaning from the pattern, the same way they do everywhere else, and the meaning has a way of following them straight into adult relationships, where it can look like over explaining every decision, apologizing for things that were never wrong, or staying somewhere unhealthy because leaving feels less survivable than staying.

The Roles Worth Naming Briefly

Certain roles show up often enough in families that they deserve to be named here, even where they belong more fully to chapters further ahead.

There is the family hero, the one who succeeds and carries the family's hopes along with the achievement, who often cannot tell the difference between failing at something and failing everyone who is counting on them. That gets a full chapter of its own later in this book.

There is the family caregiver, the one who noticed what everyone needed before they asked, who became competent early and has stayed competent ever since, and who can feel strangely uneasy on the rare occasion nobody needs anything from them at all. You have already met a version of this person, and there is a full chapter waiting for them still ahead.

And there is the family that built its identity around silence. Do not mention the money trouble. Do not talk about what happened. A family like that can teach a child, without ever saying so, that looking fine matters more than being fine, and that lesson has its own chapter later in this book as well.

THE FAMILY PEACEMAKER

If conflict was common growing up, you may have become the one who calmed the room. You learned to read a mood before anyone spoke. You softened conversations, adjusted your tone, tried never to be the reason anyone was upset.

Those are real skills, and they can make a person genuinely thoughtful and alert to others. But they can also make you feel responsible for feelings that were never yours to manage. As an adult, someone else's bad mood can still send you scrambling to fix it, even when it has nothing to do with you. You may apologize too quickly, agree when you do not actually agree, or avoid a conversation that genuinely needs to happen, all because tension itself feels dangerous.

Peace and the absence of disagreement are not the same thing. Sometimes the most loving thing in a room is the honest tension nobody wants to be the one to start.

THE FAMILY OUTSIDER

Not every inherited role comes with praise. Some people grow up feeling like the one who never quite matched the rest of the family, different in temperament, or interest, or belief, or simply in some way nobody ever bothered to name.

Some outsiders eventually build an entirely different life elsewhere. But distance does not always remove the label. A single family gathering, even decades later, can bring the old feeling straight back, and a confident adult can walk out of a childhood kitchen feeling, for a few hours, exactly twelve years old again. That does not mean the growth in between was not real. It means the old role still carries weight in that particular room, and that weight is worth naming rather than being surprised by.

WHAT FEAR CAN PASS DOWN

Roles are not the only inheritance. Sometimes what gets passed down is fear itself, of poverty, of risk, of what people will say, and it can travel much further than the event that first created it. A grandparent survives real financial hardship, and two generations later, a family that is entirely secure can still flinch at the thought of spending freely, obeying a rule whose original danger disappeared long before they were born.

This deserves real attention, more than this chapter alone can give it. A later book in this series takes up the subject of fear and anxiety directly, and that is where this thread properly belongs. For now, it is enough to notice that some of what you carry may not even be your fear to begin with.

WHAT WAS ACTUALLY GOOD

It would be unfair to this chapter, and untrue to most families, to stop here. Not everything inherited needs to be healed. Some of it only needs to be recognized and kept.

Perhaps your family taught you real perseverance, or generosity, or faith, or how to laugh at hard things without being cruel about them. These are not consolation prizes. They are genuine gifts, and this work was never about searching your past until you find something wrong with it. It is about becoming conscious enough to tell the difference between what deserves release and what deserves your gratitude, on purpose, out loud.

HONORING WITHOUT REPEATING

One of the harder truths in this chapter is that honoring where you came from does not require carrying forward everything you were given.

You can love your family and still choose differently. You can respect your parents while recognizing that a belief they held simply does not fit the life you are building. You can keep the traditions that give life and set down the ones that do not, without that being betrayal. A tree honors its roots by growing from them. Not by staying underground.

THE GUILT OF BECOMING DIFFERENT

Growth has a way of producing guilt, especially when your growth changes a pattern the whole family had quietly agreed to.

Maybe you are the first to set a real boundary, or the first to talk openly about struggling, or the first to walk away from something everyone else stayed inside of. Even healthy change unsettles people, because when one person changes, everyone around them has to adjust, whether they want to or not. Someone will eventually say, *you've changed,* and mean it as an accusation.

Maybe you have changed. The better question is what kind of change it was. Have you become less loving, or simply more honest. Less loyal, or finally more well.

REBELLION IS NOT THE SAME AS RENEWAL

It is worth being precise here, because the two get confused constantly.

Renewal is not doing the opposite of everything your family taught you, just to prove you can. That is still your family steering the car, only from the passenger seat now instead of the driver's. If they say left and you go right purely to make a point, they are still the one determining your direction.

Real freedom is quieter than that. It asks what is actually wise, what is actually true, what genuinely reflects who you are trying to become, and sometimes that answer will agree with your inheritance and sometimes it will not. The goal was never opposition. It was a choice made consciously, rather than a reaction made automatically.

THE DREAM THAT WAS NEVER YOURS

Sometimes what gets handed down is not a role or a fear, but an entire unfinished dream. A parent wanted something they never got to have, and a child grows up quietly finishing it for them.

Sometimes that dream genuinely fits, and it becomes a real inheritance worth keeping. But sometimes a person reaches midlife, successful by every visible measure, and realizes with a quiet shock that they built an entire career, or an entire life, that belonged emotionally to someone else the whole time. That realization can be painful. It can also be the beginning of something honest. You do not have to tear down what you built to ask, simply, whether the next chapter is finally allowed to be yours.

An Old Idea About Generations

There is an old thread of wisdom that runs through generations, the idea that what one family builds, or refuses to face, tends to travel forward, sometimes for a very long time. But the same wisdom insists that nobody is sentenced to repeat it forever. A different pattern can start with exactly one person, in exactly one generation, who simply decides, the fear stops here, or the silence stops here, and just as often, the faith continues here, or the generosity continues here. Healing was never about rejecting your inheritance wholesale. It is learning, piece by piece, what deserves to keep traveling forward with you.

You were given a role once, by people who mostly meant well, in circumstances that mostly required it at the time. You are allowed to outgrow it. You are allowed to become more complete than the story your family has told about you for years, and you are allowed to decide that some of what was handed to you has traveled exactly far enough.

✦

SOUL MIRROR

What role did your family hand you, and what has staying in it cost you that nobody has ever asked about?

TIMELESS WISDOM

You can honor where you came from without letting the past make every decision about where you are going. Maturity is not rejecting your inheritance. It is learning what deserves to continue.

RENEWAL PRACTICE: Keep, Question, Release

Take a page and divide it into three sections.

Under Keep, write the values, strengths, and traditions from your family you genuinely want to carry forward. Faith, generosity, hard work, hospitality, whatever is real and worth continuing.

Under Question, write the messages you are no longer certain about. *I must always be available. Strong people do not ask for help.* You do not need to resolve these today. Simply let yourself question them honestly.

Under Release, write the beliefs you can now see are doing you harm. *My needs do not matter. I am responsible for everyone's happiness.*

Then finish this sentence, and read it back slowly.

I can love where I came from without carrying everything I received.

CHAPTER FIVE

The Body You Live In

✦

HE TORE SOMETHING in his knee going up for a rebound in a Tuesday night rec league game, the kind of game that does not usually end anyone's week, let alone their sense of who they are.

The surgeon was kind and direct. Repairable, but slow, months of it, and even afterward, running the way he used to run was probably not coming back. He nodded in the office the way you nod at information you have not actually absorbed yet, and drove home, and it was not until he was sitting in his own driveway with the engine off that the actual sentence arrived.

I don't know who I am if I'm not the athletic one.

He had been that since he was twelve. Fastest kid in his grade, then the one recruited to play in college, then, for twenty years after that, the guy at the office everyone knew ran marathons, the dad who could still outrun his own kids at the park. It was never his whole personality. He had a career, a marriage, a sense of humor entirely unrelated to his legs. But underneath a great deal of it, quietly load bearing the whole time, was a body that worked exactly the way he expected it to, every single day, without asking permission first.

Now it had asked, and the answer had been no.

The Body Was Never Supposed to Carry This Much

You met a version of this idea back in the introduction to this book. Anything that can change is a dangerous place to store your entire identity, and almost nothing changes with more certainty, over a long enough life, than the body itself.

It gets injured. It gets sick. It ages, visibly and on its own schedule, regardless of what you would prefer. It does not consult you first. And if a great deal of who you believe yourself to be has been quietly resting on what this particular body could do, or how it looked doing it, every one of those changes arrives as a small earthquake, whether anyone around you notices or not.

When Appearance Becomes the Whole Report Card

Some people learn early that their looks are the thing that gets noticed first, and sometimes the thing that gets noticed almost exclusively. *You're so beautiful. You're going to break hearts.* Said with real warmth, usually, and received by a child the way most labels are received, as a description of what makes them worth something.

She was fifty six when a friend tagged her in a photo from a birthday dinner, taken from across the table without her knowing, the kind of candid shot nobody poses for. She almost scrolled past it before she realized it was her. Not because she looked unwell, or unhappy. She looked, simply, like a woman in her fifties, tired around the eyes in the particular way an honest photograph catches and a mirror, checked quickly each morning under forgiving light, generally does not.

She sat with her phone a long moment, and the thought that arrived was not really about the photograph at all. It was that she had spent her entire life, since roughly the age of seven, being the pretty one. First in the family, then at school, then in every room she walked into for three decades after that, without ever once deciding to make that her currency. It had simply been handed to her early and repeated often enough that she had stopped noticing it was doing any work at all, right up until an unposed photograph suggested that particular currency was losing value with every passing year, the way it always eventually does for everyone who has ever relied on it.

You have already seen, earlier in this book, how a compliment can quietly become a rule. This one works the same way. If beauty is what earned the attention, then aging, illness, or simply an ordinary bad photograph can start to feel like a genuine threat rather than a normal fact of being a person with a body. There is nothing wrong with wanting to look well, or taking real pleasure in your appearance. It becomes something else entirely when your appearance is the only chapter of the report your worth was ever allowed to read from.

WHEN CAPABILITY BECOMES THE WHOLE IDENTITY

The other common version is the one that found him in the driveway. Not how the body looks, but what it can do. Strong. Fast. Tireless. Able to carry the furniture, run the race, work the long shift without complaint.

This one is often praised as character rather than biology, which makes it even harder to question. Nobody tells a strong, capable person that their strength might be doing more identity work than it should. They just keep calling on it, and the person keeps supplying it, right up until a knee, or a back, or a diagnosis, declines to cooperate anymore.

It is worth noticing how closely this follows the same pattern words like *you're the strong one* set up earlier in this book, only here the label attaches to muscle and endurance instead of emotional composure. The mechanism is identical either way. A real capacity gets praised so consistently that it quietly becomes the entire basis on which a person believes they are allowed to matter, and the day that capacity falters, for any reason at all, the person underneath it discovers they never actually tested whether they were valued for anything else.

WHEN THE BODY INSISTS ON BEING NOTICED

Sometimes none of this is a slow discovery. Sometimes it arrives all at once, with a diagnosis, a chronic condition, or an injury that does not resolve on the timeline anyone hoped for. A body that had simply worked, quietly, in the background, for thirty or fifty years, suddenly demands to be thought about constantly, and there is no volunteering out of that demand.

A woman managing a chronic illness once put it simply. For years, her body was the thing that carried her to the things she cared about. Now, some mornings, her body is the thing she has to negotiate with before she can get to anything else at all, medication schedules, energy budgeted out in careful portions, plans made twice in case the first version does not hold. She did not choose that shift, and no reframing exercise was going to hand her old life back exactly as it was.

This deserves to be said plainly, because it is easy for a book like this one to sound as though the answer to every hard thing is simply a better attitude. It is not. Chronic pain is real. A frightening diagnosis is genuinely frightening, and no amount of correct thinking about identity removes the actual weight of it. What this chapter can offer is narrower than that, and it is this. Even when the body becomes the loudest thing in the room, it is still not the whole of who is in the room. The illness is real. It is not the entirety of the person carrying it, and those two things are true at exactly the same time.

If a diagnosis or a physical limitation has become the center of your own story in a way that feels too heavy to carry through reading alone, that is worth saying to a doctor, a counselor, or someone trained to help you carry it, not because you have failed at this chapter, but because some weight genuinely needs more than one pair of hands.

THE COMPARISON THAT WAITS NEARBY

It is nearly impossible to think honestly about the body without also thinking about how relentlessly it gets compared, to other people, to a photograph, to who you used to be at twenty five. That particular trap gets its own full attention shortly, later in this book, because it deserves more than a passing mention here. For now, it is enough to notice how easily the body becomes the place where comparison does its most personal work, precisely because it is the one thing about you that everyone can see without asking permission first.

THE HOUSE AND THE PERSON LIVING IN IT

Here is a distinction worth sitting with. You have a body. You are not only a body, in the sense that the body is not the entire report of who you are, even though it is the part everyone meets first.

Think of it less like a verdict and more like a house. A good house deserves real care, maintenance, attention, even pride. None of that is vanity. But a house is still where a person lives, not the person themselves, and a house changing over the years, a foundation settling, a roof needing work, does not mean the person inside it has become less real, less valuable, or less themselves. The body is the house identity happens to be living in during this particular stretch of time. It is worth caring for. It was never meant to be graded as though it were the whole score.

Two things follow from taking this seriously, and both are worth naming plainly rather than leaving implied. The first is that neglecting the house is not wisdom either. Rest, movement, decent food, a doctor's appointment you have been avoiding, these are not vanity dressed up in health language. They are simply what caring for the place you live in actually looks like, and a person who claims to have moved past caring about the body entirely is usually just avoiding one extreme by drifting into another. The second is that the house is never the whole address. Visitors remark on the house because it is what they see first, standing at the door. They stay, if they stay at all, for the person who opens it.

WHAT WAS NEVER ACTUALLY THE POINT

He did go back to the driveway question, eventually, more than once, in the months of recovery that followed. Some of what came up was genuinely hard, real grief for a version of moving through the world he was not getting back in quite the same form.

But somewhere in that same stretch of months, sitting still in ways his body had never really allowed before, he noticed something he had not expected to find. He was still funny. Still good at his job, in a way that had nothing to do with his legs. Still exactly the father his kids wanted at the dinner table, even on nights he could not get down on the floor with them. None of that had required a working knee to begin with. It had simply been standing quietly behind the running the entire time, waiting to be noticed.

She kept the photograph, in the end, instead of deleting it, and found herself looking at it again a few weeks later with something closer to curiosity than dread. The tiredness around the eyes was real. So, she noticed, was everything the tiredness had actually cost to earn, thirty years of raising a family, building a career people respected, staying up late with friends going through hard seasons of their own. A face changes because a life happened to it. That had always seemed like a loss when she thought about it late at night. Looked at in the middle of an ordinary afternoon, it looked considerably more like evidence.

Neither of them lost anything essential in the moment their body stopped cooperating with the old terms. What they lost was a particular measuring stick, the one that had been quietly running the whole time without either of them fully choosing it. The body will keep changing for as long as you are alive to have one. That was never actually optional, for you or for anyone else reading this. What is worth deciding, now, is how much of your worth you are willing to let it carry.

✦

SOUL MIRROR

If your body could no longer do the thing you are proudest of it doing, who would still be standing there?

TIMELESS WISDOM

You are not only the body you live in. You are the person who lives in it, and that person does not disappear simply because the body changes.

RENEWAL PRACTICE: What My Body Has Carried

Take a page and write down five moments across your life when your body made something possible, not how it looked in the moment, but what it allowed you to do or be present for.

Holding someone. Walking somewhere that mattered. Recovering from something that once seemed impossible to survive. Simply showing up, on an ordinary day, for someone who needed you there.

Read the list back. Notice how few of the entries are about appearance, and how many are about presence, service, and simply being there for something that mattered.

That list is a truer account of what your body has actually been for than any mirror has ever offered you.

CHAPTER SIX

Words That Became Your Identity

✦

HE IS FIFTY two years old and he still remembers four words.

He cannot tell you what the assignment was. He could not describe the classroom, or say what time of year it was, or pick the teacher out of a lineup. All of that is gone, the way almost everything from that age is gone.

But he can tell you the four words, in order, in her handwriting, in red.

This is lazy work.

He is an architect now. He is good at it. He also checks every drawing four times before it leaves his desk, and then once more in the evening, and sometimes once again in the morning before anybody else arrives. His colleagues think he is thorough. His wife thinks he is tired.

He does not connect any of it to a piece of paper handed back in a classroom forty years ago. Why would he? That was a Tuesday. That was nothing.

But sometimes, in the last hour before a deadline, when the tiredness gets in, a sentence surfaces in his mind without being invited.

You are lazy and everybody is about to find out.

It used to arrive in her voice.

Somewhere along the way, at a moment he could not possibly identify, it started arriving in his own.

Words get in.

That is the whole of this chapter, and everything that follows is only detail. Something is said about you, usually by somebody whose opinion mattered at the time, and if the conditions are right, that sentence does not stay outside where it belongs. It comes inside. It takes up residence. And after enough years it stops sounding like somebody's opinion of you and starts sounding like a simple description of reality.

Here is how it happens, step by step, because it is worth seeing the mechanism laid out plainly.

Somebody says something.

You decide what it means about you. This part happens fast, usually in less than a second, and almost never consciously.

You start to believe it.

You begin repeating it to yourself, in your own voice, without noticing that you have taken over the job.

You act in ways that fit the belief. You avoid what you now think you are bad at. You over prepare where you think you are weak. You do not apply.

And then life produces results that match, which you take as proof.

By the end of that chain, the sentence looks like evidence. It looks like something you worked out about yourself through years of honest observation. It is not. It is something you were handed at nine, and everything since has been you gathering support for it.

But notice the second step, because that is where the freedom is.

Somebody says something. Then *you decide what it means.*

That is the hinge. And it explains something that otherwise makes no sense.

Two children can hear exactly the same sentence and walk away with completely different lives.

A father says to both his sons, on separate occasions, the same seven words. *You need to work harder than that.*

The older boy hears a challenge. He was already fairly sure his father thought well of him, so the sentence lands on top of that certainty and becomes something almost warm. *He thinks I'm capable of more.* He works harder. He remembers it later as the moment somebody believed in him.

The younger boy hears a verdict. He has spent his whole childhood watching his brother and quietly concluding that he is the disappointing one, and the sentence lands on top of *that.* It does not sound like a challenge. It sounds like confirmation. *He's noticed. He's finally saying it out loud.*

Same father. Same words. Same tone, most likely. Two entirely different sentences, because they landed in two different places.

This matters for two reasons.

The first is that it lets some people off the hook. Not everyone who shaped you was trying to. A good deal of the damage in this book was done by people who meant no harm at all and would be genuinely distressed to learn what a passing remark became.

The second reason is harder, and it is the important one. If interpretation is where the sentence gets its power, then interpretation is also where it can be taken back.

You cannot unsay what was said to you.

You can absolutely revisit what you decided it meant.

Now we have to be careful, because there is a version of this teaching that does real damage, and it is everywhere.

It goes like this. Words are powerful, therefore all difficult words are harmful, therefore anybody who says something that hurts is doing you an injury and should be removed from your life.

That is not what this chapter says. That is not true, and living by it will leave you surrounded by people who tell you only what you want to hear, which is a lonelier and more dangerous place than it sounds.

Some of the most valuable sentences of my life have been uncomfortable ones. Certain people loved me enough to tell me things I did not want to hear, at some cost to themselves, and I am better for it. A friend who will not tell you the truth is pleasant company and not much else.

So the question is not whether a sentence was comfortable.

The question is what the sentence was about.

Hold these two next to each other.

If you keep spending more than you earn, you are going to find yourself in serious trouble.

You are useless with money. You always have been. You will never amount to anything.

Both are unwelcome. Both might be said in the same tone of voice, at the same kitchen table, by the same person, on the same evening.

But look at what each one is actually describing.

The first describes something you are doing. It names a pattern, it names where the pattern leads, and it leaves the door open, because a thing you are doing is a thing you can stop doing. It assumes there is a version of you on the other side of this who has changed. It is unpleasant to hear and it is fundamentally hopeful.

The second describes something you are. Not a behavior. A nature. And you cannot stop being your nature. There is no door in that sentence. There is nothing to do with it except carry it.

That is the difference between correction and condemnation, and once you can see it you will see it everywhere.

Correction speaks to what you did. Condemnation attacks who you are.

You made a poor decision and *you are a fool* are not two strengths of the same sentence. They are two different kinds of sentence entirely. One is information. The other is a sentence in the legal meaning of the word, something handed down, something to be served.

There is a simple test, and you can run it in a second on anything anybody says to you, including the things you say to yourself.

Can the thing being described be changed?

If yes, it is correction. It may be badly delivered. It may be poorly timed. It may have been said in anger by somebody with no right to say it. But it is still, structurally, about something changeable, and there is something you can do with it.

If no, it is not information about you. It is somebody's verdict, and verdicts can be appealed.

Learning to receive correction without turning it into condemnation may be one of the most useful skills a person can develop. It is what allows you to hear something difficult, take the part that is true, act on it, and remain intact. Without it, every piece of feedback becomes a referendum on your worth, and so you start avoiding feedback, and once you are avoiding feedback you have stopped growing.

Now for the part people do not expect.

Not every sentence that shapes a life sounds unkind.

You are the strong one.

You never give us any trouble.

You are the clever one in this family.

Everybody depends on you.

You always get it right.

Every one of those was said with love. Most were said with pride. If you asked the person who said it, they would tell you, correctly, that they were praising a child.

But listen to what a child hears underneath.

You are the strong one can arrive as *so do not be anything else.*

You never give us any trouble can arrive as *and we would rather you didn't start.*

You are the clever one can arrive as *your value here is your marks.*

Praise binds a person exactly as tightly as criticism does, and it is harder to see, because who complains about being praised? The strong one grows up frightened of being weak. The clever one grows up terrified of failing. The one who never gave any trouble grows up unable to say what they need. The dependable one feels guilty on a day off.

These are not people who were mistreated. Many of them had loving homes. They were simply handed a description early, and they have been living inside it ever since, and nobody, including them, has ever thought to ask whether it fits.

Sometimes the damage runs the other way entirely. It is not what was said. It is what never was.

I am proud of you. I love you. I believe in you. You did well.

Some people grew up with food, shelter, discipline, and a genuinely decent home, and still spent their childhood a little hungry for four or five sentences nobody ever got around to saying out loud. This does not necessarily mean the love was missing. Some people love enormously and were never taught how to say so. A father who works sixteen hour days for thirty years to keep his family fed has proven something real about love, even if the words themselves never once left his mouth. Both things can be true at once, the love was genuine and the hunger was real, and understanding what you needed does not require you to deny what you actually received.

Not every wound arrives shouted, either. Some of the most durable ones arrive laughing.

A nickname that will not die. A joke about your weight that gets repeated at every family gathering for fifteen years. A running bit about how slow you were at school. Nobody at the table thinks of it as cruelty. It is simply the joke now, the one everybody expects, and the person it is aimed at has usually learned to laugh along, because laughing along is easier than explaining, again, that it stopped being funny around the third telling. Context and relationship genuinely matter here, and healthy families do tease each other without doing harm. But if the same joke keeps landing on the same old bruise, it is worth someone finally asking, gently, whether it is actually still funny, or whether it simply became furniture nobody thought to move.

Which brings us to the voice you are living with now.

Because the difficult truth is that most of the sentences doing damage in your life today are not being said by anybody. Everyone who originally said them may be elderly, or estranged, or dead. The teacher who wrote four words in red has almost certainly forgotten it. She may have written something similar on twenty papers that week.

The sentence lives on anyway, because you took over.

Listen to what you say to yourself when you drop something. When you get a date wrong. When you catch sight of yourself unexpectedly. When you send the message and immediately wish you had not.

Most people, if they are honest, will find that they speak to themselves in a way they would not tolerate from a stranger and would not dream of using on a child.

And here is the question I want to leave you with, because it changes things.

Where did you learn to talk like that?

Nobody comes up with it on their own. Self criticism is a learned accent. You picked it up from somewhere, and if you sit still long enough, you can usually hear whose it originally was.

There is an old proverb that says the tongue holds the power of life and death. It has been quoted for thousands of years, usually as a warning about gossip. I think it is more literal than that, and slower.

Words spoken over a child do not simply hurt for an afternoon. They get installed. They become the voice in a fifty two year old architect's head at eleven at night. They decide who applies and who does not, who marries and who stays alone, who tries and who never risks it.

That is life and death, spread out over decades, and delivered a sentence at a time.

One honest caveat belongs here before we go further. Some words go beyond ordinary hurt. Repeated humiliation, threats, and language designed specifically to make a person doubt their own judgment or their ability to function on their own are not simply an unkind version of what this chapter has been describing. That is something heavier, and its effects can run deeper than a book, on its own, can safely undo. If that describes something in your history, the right next step is very often a qualified counselor or therapist rather than another chapter, and reaching for that kind of help is not a failure to heal on your own. It is usually the wisest move available.

For most of us, most of the time, the work is smaller than that, though no less real. It is simply learning to ask, honestly, which of the sentences we carry were ever true, and which ones we only ever inherited.

There is one more caution worth adding, because it runs in the opposite direction. Words matter enormously, but they are not magic. Saying *I am wealthy* on repeat does not deposit money into an account, and insisting *I will never get sick* does not replace rest, medicine, or wisdom. Words shape the beliefs, decisions, and habits that shape a life. They do not substitute for living it. Treating language as a spell is its own kind of trap, just a more hopeful sounding one, and this chapter is not asking you to trade one distortion for another.

Before we close, the mirror is worth turning around, because this chapter has mostly asked what words did to you, and there is a second question underneath it that matters just as much.

What are your words doing to the people who hear them.

Your children hear you. So does your spouse, and the people you work alongside, and anyone who has ever come to you needing something honest. It is worth asking, plainly, whether your words tend to correct behavior while leaving a person's dignity intact, or whether *always* and *never* creep in whenever you are angry enough to reach for them. It is worth asking whether you have ever needed to apologize for something cruel you said and never quite got around to it. None of this is meant to produce guilt. It is meant to produce responsibility, and responsibility is simply the part of this chapter that was always going to include you as the speaker, not only as the one who was spoken to.

You are allowed to find out which of the sentences you carry were ever true. And the people closest to you deserve the same care with the sentences you hand to them.

✦

SOUL MIRROR

Whose voice is it, really, when you criticize yourself?

TIMELESS WISDOM

Correction speaks to what you did. Condemnation attacks who you are. Wisdom knows the difference and refuses to confuse the two.

RENEWAL PRACTICE: The Sentence Audit

Write down three things you say to yourself when you are under pressure. Word for word, exactly as they arrive, including the unkind parts. Do not tidy them up.

Then take each one and ask three questions.

Who said it first? Sit with this longer than feels necessary. The answer is often somebody you have not thought about in years.

What was it originally about? There was usually a real event underneath. A test. A job. A conversation. Find it if you can.

Does it describe something I did, or something I am?

Now rewrite each sentence as correction. Name the behavior. Leave a way forward. Say it the way you would say it to somebody you loved who had made the same mistake.

Then read both versions out loud, one after the other.

You will hear the difference. That is the point. You have been reading only one of them for a very long time, and it helps to hear how it sounds next to the alternative.

CHAPTER SEVEN

When Other People's Opinions Become Your Mirror

✦

SHE SENT THE text at 9:14 and watched the three dots appear almost immediately.

Then they disappeared.

Then they appeared again, and disappeared again, and she sat there on the edge of the bed replaying the message she had sent, a fairly ordinary opinion about a fairly ordinary plan, looking for the sentence in it that must have been wrong. By 9:26 she had rewritten the entire conversation in her head four different ways, in three of which she came across as pushy, and had nearly typed *sorry, ignore that, it's not a big deal* before an actual reply finally landed. *Sounds great, was just making dinner!*

Nothing had happened. Twelve minutes of a friend cooking pasta had produced twelve minutes of quiet, private trial.

Most people carry some version of this, and there is nothing unusual about it. We are social by nature, built for relationship, and other people's responses were never supposed to be irrelevant to us. The trouble is not that their opinions matter. The trouble is when their opinions become the only mirror we check, so that approval starts to feel like proof of our value and disapproval starts to feel like proof of the opposite, and somewhere in there the question quietly changes from *what is true about me* to *what do they currently think about me.*

The Need to Be Seen

There is something entirely human in wanting to be seen, not merely noticed, but actually known and valued by the people who matter to you. A child looks toward a parent asking, without words, *do you see me.* An adult looks toward a spouse still wondering, twenty years in, *do you still choose me.* None of that is a flaw. Wanting to be seen is part of what makes us capable of real connection at all.

It becomes something else when being seen and being valuable quietly merge into the same thing, so that the soul starts running on whatever the room happens to be reflecting back that day.

Approval Feels Good, and That Is Not the Problem

Let's say this plainly. Approval feels good, and there is nothing wrong with enjoying it. *You did well. I'm proud of you. You handled that wisely.* None of that needs to be treated with suspicion.

The real question is not whether you enjoy approval. It is whether you need it in order to feel steady. There is a real difference between *I appreciate your approval* and *I need your approval to feel okay about myself,* and most people, if they are honest, can feel exactly which side of that line a given relationship sits on.

The Person Who Reads the Room for a Living

Some people spend most of a conversation not listening to it, but scanning it. Did I say too much. Are they upset with me. Why haven't they responded yet. The room becomes a constant stream of information, tone, silence, a slow reply, a short one, and every signal gets processed for what it might mean about whether things are still okay.

This happens because the person is not simply reading the room. They are reading themselves through it. If the room seems pleased, they feel safe. If someone goes quiet, they start filling in the silence with the worst available explanation. It is an exhausting way to move through an ordinary day, and most people who do it have been doing it so long they no longer notice the effort involved.

WHEN REJECTION OUTGROWS THE MOMENT

Rejection hurts, and it can hurt even when your own logic knows better. But the sharpest part of it is rarely the event itself. It is what the event seems to be saying underneath.

I wasn't chosen becomes *I am not good enough. They didn't invite me* becomes *they don't actually value me.* The event is real. The larger conclusion usually is not, or at least is not proven by the small thing that triggered it, and rejection tends to hit hardest exactly where it lands on an older bruise rather than where the actual damage is.

This is also where a small moment has a habit of turning into a much bigger verdict. One person's criticism becomes *people don't like me.* One friendship ending becomes *nobody stays.* Notice the word doing the damage in both of those sentences. One becomes people. One becomes nobody. Certainty feels better than uncertainty, so the mind often reaches for the widest possible version of events, even though the widest version is almost never the true one. One person's opinion, however painful, is still only one person's opinion.

WHAT PLEASING PEOPLE IS OFTEN COVERING

Not all agreeableness comes from fear, and this chapter is not asking you to treat every yes with suspicion. But some of it does, and it is worth being honest about the shape it takes. *If they're unhappy, I've failed. If I say no, they might stop loving me.* That is a genuinely heavy way to move through a life, saying yes to things you have no capacity for, softening opinions you actually hold, staying quiet in conversations that need your honest voice.

This has its own chapter waiting further ahead in this book, because the person who cannot say no deserves more than a paragraph. For now, it is enough to notice whether any of this sounds like you, and to know that a fuller answer is coming.

You Will Disappoint People

This might be the hardest sentence in the whole chapter, so it is worth stating plainly rather than softening it. You will disappoint people. Even doing your best. Even being kind. You will say no, change your mind, take a different path, need rest, end something that was no longer working, and not everyone will understand it the way you hoped they would.

Some will call it selfishness. Some will simply say you've changed, and mean it as a complaint rather than an observation. Often what has actually changed is that you have become harder to use and easier to know, and for someone who benefited from the older, more accommodating version of you, that can genuinely feel like a loss on their end, even while it is real growth on yours.

Not Every Hard Word Is Wrong

We already spent real time, a chapter ago, on the difference between a hard truth and an unfair verdict, correction that names something you did against condemnation that claims to name something you are. The same test applies here. Someone telling you that you interrupt too often, or promise more than you deliver, might be handing you something genuinely useful, uncomfortable as it feels to receive.

Healthy identity does not mean deciding you no longer care what anyone thinks. That is not freedom. It is just a different kind of rigidity. It means learning to listen carefully without handing every single opinion automatic authority over your worth.

Who Actually Gets a Vote

Not every opinion deserves equal weight, and one of the more useful questions you can ask is simply who has actually earned the right to speak deeply into your life. A friend who has known you for fifteen years and wants your good deserves more weight than a stranger's passing comment. Someone who tells you the truth because they love you deserves more than someone who only ever flatters you.

Most people never sort this consciously. They give equal weight to every voice in the room, the wise ones and the careless ones alike, simply because all of them arrived as opinions. Sorting them on purpose is most of the work of this chapter.

A NUMBER ON A SCREEN

Modern life has quietly turned approval into arithmetic, likes, views, shares, and it is worth naming honestly how much power those small numbers can carry even when we know, intellectually, that they shouldn't. One post does well and you feel sharper, more interesting, more like yourself. The next one barely moves and something in you deflates a little, for no reason you could defend out loud.

There is an entire chapter further ahead dedicated to exactly this, the self a person builds specifically for a screen, and what happens when that self starts running the whole show. For now, simply notice that the danger was never the platform itself. It is letting a public number quietly become a private verdict.

EXPLAINING YOURSELF INTO THE GROUND

One reliable sign of approval dependence is the impulse to over explain. You make a decision, and then you find yourself justifying it again, and again, hoping that if people just understood clearly enough, they would finally approve.

But sometimes people understand you completely and still disagree, and that is a genuinely hard thing to sit with. You can explain yourself with total clarity and still disappoint someone. Maturity includes learning that being understood imperfectly does not have to knock you off your footing.

Learning to Tolerate Disappointing Someone

This is a skill, not a personality trait, which means it can actually be built. It is the ability to let someone be upset without racing to fix it. To hear real disagreement without collapsing. To say, evenly, *I understand you see this differently,* and mean it, without following it up with three more sentences trying to win them back over.

It rarely comes naturally, especially to anyone who once learned that disagreement threatened the whole relationship. But it is learnable, the same way any skill is, through small doses and repeated practice rather than one dramatic breakthrough.

What Steadiness Actually Looks Like

A secure sense of self does not make a person hard to reach. It makes them steady. Praise does not go to their head, because their head was never resting on it in the first place. Criticism does not flatten them, because it was never the foundation either. This is not coldness. It is closer to what an anchor does, invisible most of the time, doing its quiet work exactly when the water gets rough. There is a fuller picture of this kind of steadiness waiting near the very end of this book, because it takes the whole journey to build properly. This chapter is simply the first real look at it.

A life built entirely on being well received will always be a fragile life, because people change their minds, moods shift, and rooms that loved you yesterday can go cold for reasons that have nothing to do with you at all. A steadier foundation has to be anchored somewhere other people cannot reach, and that is really the whole argument of this book, chapter by chapter.

Other people will always reflect something back at you, admiration, disappointment, misunderstanding, real love. You cannot control what gets reflected. But you get to decide how much authority each reflection is given, and that decision, made quietly and repeatedly, is one of the truer freedoms available to you.

✦

SOUL MIRROR

Whose disappointment is hardest for you to tolerate, and what do you fear it would actually mean about you?

TIMELESS WISDOM

You can value other people's opinions without making them the final authority on your worth. Feedback can guide you. Approval can encourage you. But neither one was ever meant to be the foundation you stand on.

RENEWAL PRACTICE: Who Gets a Vote

Write three headings on a page.

Under *Voices I Trust,* list the people who know you well, love you honestly, and genuinely want your growth.

Under *Voices I Consider,* list people whose feedback may be useful sometimes, but whose opinion does not define you either way.

Under *Voices I Have Given Too Much Power,* list anyone, named or general, whose approval or criticism currently affects you more than it reasonably should.

For each name in that third column, ask yourself honestly why they were given that much room. Then write one sentence and read it back slowly.

I can listen without surrendering myself.

CHAPTER EIGHT

Comparison and the Manufactured Self

✦

AT EIGHT IN the morning she was, by any honest measure, content.

Coffee, a slow start, the kitchen doing what kitchens do. Then she picked up her phone, the way people do before they've fully decided to, and scrolled for a while. A friend's new kitchen, gleaming and enormous. Someone's beach vacation, four days in and every photo perfect. A former colleague's promotion, announced with the kind of humility that somehow makes it land harder.

By eight fifteen, the same kitchen looked smaller. The same coffee tasted like something she was settling for. Nothing in her actual life had changed in those fifteen minutes. Not her house, her job, her family, her bank account. Only what she had been looking at had changed, and somehow that was enough to quietly rearrange how she felt about everything she already had.

That is the strange power of comparison. It can alter how you feel about your life without laying a finger on your life itself.

Comparison Is Human, Until It Isn't

Everyone compares. Children compare toys. Adults compare careers, homes, marriages, children, and a dozen other things before lunch. Comparison, at its most basic, is simply information, a way of understanding where you stand, and it can even be useful. Watching someone do something well and thinking *I could learn from that* is a healthy use of the instinct.

It turns into something else the moment it stops delivering information and starts delivering a verdict. Someone else's success becomes evidence of your failure. Their happiness becomes a question mark over yours. At that point you are no longer observing another person's life. You are using it to measure your own worth, and the two were never meant to be the same operation.

The Measuring Stick Keeps Moving

Comparison has a maddening habit of relocating the finish line right as you reach it. You wanted the degree, and you got it, and now somebody has two. You wanted the business, and you built it, and now somebody's is larger. You reached ten thousand followers and discovered somebody else has a million.

It never once says *congratulations, you have arrived, you may rest now.* It simply moves.

Someone Will Always Be Ahead

This is simply true, and no amount of achievement changes it. Someone will always be younger, richer, more accomplished, more admired by whatever standard happens to be fashionable this year. If your peace requires being the best person in every room you enter, peace will always be just out of reach, because even the top of one mountain reveals another one behind it. A secure identity can genuinely admire excellence in someone else without needing to personally own all of it.

The Manufactured Self

Comparison becomes dangerous the moment it starts producing a version of you built specifically to compete rather than a version of you built to actually live. You buy something you cannot really afford because of what it signals. You stay in a relationship you have outgrown because ending it would dent how your life looks from the outside. You pretend to be busier, happier, and more comfortable than you actually are.

Slowly the life stops being lived and starts being presented. You are no longer simply existing. You are producing evidence, that you are doing well, that you have not fallen behind, that you still matter. That production is the manufactured self, and it is exhausting in a way that never quite announces itself as exhaustion.

There is nothing wrong with presenting yourself well, dressing with care, or sharing something you're proud of. The real question is what happens the moment the presentation becomes more important than the life underneath it. Someone deeply in debt who keeps spending because they cannot bear looking unsuccessful. A couple whose marriage is quietly failing while they invest real energy in appearing perfect at every gathering. The appearance of a good life has taken over the actual work of building one, and that is an expensive trade no matter how it photographs.

WE ONLY COMPARE WHAT CAN BE SEEN

Part of what makes comparison so misleading is that most of what actually matters cannot be seen at all. You see the house, not the mortgage pressure behind it. You see the wedding photograph, not the marriage that follows it. You see the promotion, not what it cost the person to get there.

None of this means every successful person is secretly miserable. That would just be comparison running in the opposite direction. Some people really are doing wonderfully, and they deserve to be celebrated rather than quietly suspected. The point is simpler than that. You are almost never seeing the whole story, so building a verdict about your own life out of a fragment of somebody else's is a shaky foundation no matter which direction it points.

A Word on Screens

Comparison did not begin with a phone in anyone's hand. Neighbors compared farms long before that. But screens gave it constant access, and gave us something new to compare ourselves against, not real people we actually know, but their single best photograph from their single best hour. There is a full chapter further ahead built specifically around the self a person constructs for a screen, and what happens when that self quietly takes over. For now, it is enough to notice that ordinary life was never going to win against someone else's highlight reel. It was never a fair fight to begin with.

The Body, Measured Against Someone Else's

Appearance invites comparison as easily as anything does, and the standard has a way of shifting every few years regardless of who meets it. If the ideal itself keeps changing, that alone should tell you it is not a safe place to store your worth. There is nothing wrong with wanting to look well and take care of yourself. It becomes something else entirely the moment looking different from somebody else starts to feel like being worth less than them.

Relationships, Measured the Same Way

Everyone else seems to be getting married, having children, thriving, right on schedule, while your own life is unfolding on a different timetable entirely, or not unfolding the way you had hoped at all. Comparison has a habit of turning another person's genuine blessing into evidence that something is wrong with you specifically. It rarely is. Their marriage does not make your singleness a failure. Their children's success does not make you a failed parent. You are allowed to want something deeply without treating its absence as a verdict on your worth.

WHEN IT HAPPENS BETWEEN FRIENDS

This is where comparison gets genuinely uncomfortable, because it can arrive right alongside real love for someone. You are happy for your friend, and something in you still hurts when their good news lands. Both things can be true in the same breath, and the mature response is not pretending the sting isn't there. It is asking what their success seems to be saying about you. *I'm behind. I should have gotten there by now.* Once you can hear that sentence clearly, you have usually found the real conversation. It was rarely about your friend at all.

WHAT ENVY IS ACTUALLY TELLING YOU

Envy is uncomfortable to admit, but it is rarely just noise. It often points at something real, a desire you quietly abandoned, an insecurity worth naming, a place where you genuinely feel life has been unfair to you. Instead of immediately being ashamed of the feeling, it is worth asking what it might be pointing toward. Someone else's freedom might be reminding you how boxed in you feel. Someone else's confidence might be revealing how much you doubt your own. The goal is never to feed the envy. It is to hear what it is trying to tell you, and then decide, honestly, what part of that message actually belongs to you.

COMPARING YOURSELF TO YOURSELF

Not every comparison points outward. Sometimes the person you cannot stop measuring yourself against is a younger, healthier, or simply different version of you, before the loss, before the diagnosis, before the children left the house. *I used to be somebody* is a genuinely painful thought, and the person you were deserves real appreciation. But your own past should not become one more mirror informing your present self that it has lost value. Life moves in seasons, some for building and some for releasing, and different does not automatically mean less.

There is a nearby cousin of this comparison, aimed not at who you were but at who you expected to be by now. *I thought I'd be married by now. I thought the business would be bigger.* Sometimes what actually needs grieving is not somebody else's life, but the life you once expected to be living at this exact age, and that grief deserves honesty rather than dismissal. An unmet timeline is not the same thing as a meaningless one. Your life is happening now, not inside the schedule you wrote for it twenty years ago.

Behind, According to Whom

This question is worth asking directly whenever it surfaces. Behind whom, exactly. According to whose schedule. Some deadlines carry genuine weight, and this book will not pretend timing never matters. But a great many of the deadlines we feel most acutely are simply social ones, everyone else did it, my family expected it, and therefore I should already be there too. Maybe. Often, though, that math was never really yours to begin with.

Learning From Someone, Without Needing to Become Them

There is a healthy way to look at another person's life, and it sounds different from comparison even though the two can be easy to confuse. *I admire her discipline. I want to understand how they built that.* That is learning, and it asks what principle might be worth applying. Comparison asks a much narrower question, why am I not that person, and that question rarely expands anyone. It mostly just erases them a little at a time.

Your path will not look like theirs, because your history, your resources, and your timing are not theirs either. That is not injustice. It is simply what it means to be a different person walking a different road, and it does not disqualify anything you learn along the way from being genuinely useful.

WHEN COMPARISON MAKES YOU ABANDON WHAT WAS WORKING

This happens quietly and often goes unnoticed until much later. You are building something steadily, and then you see someone growing faster by a different method, so you switch. Then somebody else appears to be succeeding a third way, and you switch again. Eventually you realize you have abandoned real, working progress more than once simply because somebody else's progress looked more impressive from the outside.

Not everything meaningful happens quickly. Roots, in particular, tend to grow in the exact places nobody is applauding.

THE FREEDOM TO CELEBRATE SOMEONE ELSE

One genuine sign of growing security is the ability to watch someone else succeed and feel glad, without needing to first check whether it costs you anything. Their beauty does not steal yours. Their opportunity does not use up whatever was left over for you. Another person's light was never a threat to yours, and it takes real practice to feel that as true rather than just agreeing with it as a sentence.

THE FREEDOM TO BE ORDINARY

There is a freedom worth naming that gets very little attention. The freedom to simply be ordinary, some of the time, without turning it into anything else. Not every meal needs documenting. Not every hobby needs to become income. Not every quiet Saturday needs proof that it happened.

Some of the best parts of a life were never meant to be witnessed by anyone but the person living them. A walk. A conversation. A garden nobody photographs. A life does not require an audience in order to have actually mattered.

WHAT IS ACTUALLY YOURS

Comparison keeps asking what someone else has. A steadier question underneath it is simpler and considerably more useful. What has actually been given into your hands. What abilities, what relationships, what season, what resources, what particular set of circumstances is genuinely yours to build with right now.

You cannot build an effective life while spending most of your attention trying to live somebody else's, and contentment with what you currently hold is not the same thing as giving up on growing it. You are allowed to be grateful for your life and still be actively working to improve it. Those are not opposites. They were never meant to be.

WHAT CANNOT REST

The manufactured self has to be maintained constantly, kept looking successful, kept appearing happy, kept proving something to a room that may not even be paying attention. The self underneath it, the one not built for comparison, can actually rest. Not because there is nothing left to grow. There will always be more of that. But growth stops needing to start from *I must become someone else to matter,* and starts, instead, from something considerably more peaceful. I can become a fuller, wiser version of the one life that was actually given to me.

✦

SOUL MIRROR

When you see someone else's success, what is the very first sentence your mind says about you?

TIMELESS WISDOM

Someone else's life can inspire you without becoming the ruler you use to measure your own. You can admire without imitating, learn without disappearing, and celebrate someone else's success without quietly using it as evidence against yourself.

RENEWAL PRACTICE: The Comparison Audit

For the next seven days, notice whenever comparison shifts your mood, and simply record it without judging yourself for it.

Write down who or what you saw, what you immediately thought about yourself in response, and what you suddenly felt you needed to change, buy, achieve, or prove.

Then ask one question of each entry. Did I actually want this before I made the comparison?

Sometimes the honest answer is yes, and that is useful information, a real goal comparison happened to surface. But sometimes you will notice something else entirely. I was genuinely content until I saw someone else's life.

When that happens, it helps to remind yourself plainly. Their life is information. It was never an instruction.

Then return to yours.

CHAPTER NINE

The Curated Self

✦

THE PHOTO WAS from a trip they took two summers ago, both of them laughing on a boat somewhere the light was doing something spectacular, and she had scheduled it to post on their anniversary months in advance, back when scheduling it felt like a nice thing to do for future her.

By the time it actually posted, they had been separated for six weeks.

She thought about deleting it. She did not, mostly because deleting it felt like it would require an explanation she was not ready to give anyone yet, and by ten that morning the comments had already started arriving. *Relationship goals. You two are the best. Happy anniversary to my favorite couple.* She read each one standing in her kitchen, alone, and typed a heart in reply to most of them, because that was faster than the truth and nobody had actually asked for the truth.

This is not a story about dishonesty. She was not lying, exactly. That photograph was completely real, the laughter was real, the light on the water was real. It simply was not this morning, and this morning was the only one that was actually true.

The Self Built for an Audience

Every one of us presents some version of ourselves to other people, and earlier in this book we spent real time on that gap, the self other people meet and the self that exists when nobody is checking. What makes the curated self different is not the gap itself. It is the audience, and the permanence, and the fact that the version being presented can now be built, edited, scheduled, and revised until it says exactly what you intended, in a way no live conversation ever allows.

That is not automatically a problem. There is nothing wrong with sharing something you are proud of, documenting a life you are genuinely glad to be living, or simply enjoying the small pleasure of a nice photograph landing well. The question this chapter is actually asking is narrower than that. What happens when the curated version stops being a highlight of your life and starts being the version you are most responsible to.

TWO SELVES, SLOWLY DRIFTING APART

At first the gap between the posted life and the lived one is small, the ordinary difference between a highlight reel and an ordinary Tuesday. Everyone understands that a vacation photo does not include the argument in the car on the way to the airport. Nobody expects otherwise.

The gap tends to widen quietly, though, the same way most identity patterns in this book widen, without a single dramatic moment marking the shift. A rough week gets left off entirely, not because it was hidden on purpose, but because it simply did not fit the account's tone. A milestone gets posted a little early, or held a little late, until it lands at the most flattering possible moment. None of these choices feel dishonest individually. Collectively, over years, they can produce two versions of a life running on separate tracks, one that gets witnessed and one that actually gets lived, and the person maintaining both can start to feel a strange, specific loneliness that is difficult to explain to anyone, because from the outside their life looks completely fine.

This particular loneliness is worth naming precisely, because it does not resemble ordinary isolation. The person experiencing it is often surrounded by real friends, a genuine community, warm comments arriving regularly from people who care about them. What is missing is not company. It is the experience of being known in the moment something actually happened, rather than known only through a version of it edited and released later, once the rough edges had already been smoothed away. A friend who only ever meets the edited account is, in a very real sense, one version of intimacy behind the person they think they know well.

When the Numbers Start Grading You

We already looked at how quickly a like or a comment can start functioning as a private verdict rather than simple information. What is worth adding here is what happens once that verdict starts shaping what gets posted in the first place.

A certain kind of photo performs well, so more of that kind gets taken. A certain kind of caption, a certain kind of honesty, a certain kind of humor, earns warmth, and the account quietly starts producing more of whatever earns it. This is not unusual or particularly sinister. It is simply how attention works, and most platforms are built to reward exactly this cycle. But somewhere inside that cycle, a person can lose track of whether they are documenting a life they are actually living, or manufacturing content calibrated to a response they have started needing.

The Maintenance Never Really Stops

A curated identity, once it reaches a certain size, requires upkeep the way any performance does. The tone has to stay consistent. The version of the marriage, the career, the body, the family, that has already been established has to keep being true, or at least keep looking true, because an account that has spent two years posting a certain kind of life has an audience that now expects it.

This is part of why the woman with the anniversary photo did not simply post the truth that morning. It was not cowardice. It was that an entire established account, built over years, was suddenly at odds with what was actually happening, and there was no simple caption available that could hold both things at once. Maintaining a curated self is quiet, constant labor, and very few people budget for how much of it there actually is until a moment like that one forces the bill into view.

WHEN THE SELF IS BUILT FROM SCRATCH, ON PURPOSE

Not every curated self starts as an accidental drift from an ordinary life. Some are built deliberately, from the very first post, and it is worth looking at that version too, because it shows the same mechanism operating at full strength, without any of the accidental softness a personal account usually has.

She was nineteen when she started posting about her morning routine, her workouts, the meals she prepared with careful natural light, and within a year she had built something that looked, from the outside, like an entire identity, calm, disciplined, glowing. People messaged her regularly to say she had changed their lives. She read every message and meant every reply, and most days the account did genuinely reflect something true about how she was trying to live.

The trouble arrived on the days it did not. A bad week, a body that did not cooperate, a morning that started with tears instead of a green smoothie, none of it had anywhere to go, because the account had never once shown a version of her having a bad week, and introducing one now felt less like honesty and more like a betrayal of everyone who had come to rely on the calm, glowing version to feel calmer themselves. She began quietly avoiding the platform on her hardest days, not because she was hiding anything new, but because the version of herself she had spent a year building had no room left in it for anything except going well.

She was, in a very real sense, competing with an earlier version of herself, one built entirely out of her own best mornings, stitched together into something no single day could ever actually match.

What Gets Lost in the Editing

The specific danger of a curated self is not that it is untrue. Most of it, taken piece by piece, usually is true. The danger is more particular than that. It is that the edited version, repeated often enough, can start to feel like the only version worth having, so that an ordinary, unphotogenic, unremarkable stretch of real life, most of which is exactly that, starts to feel like it does not count.

A quiet Tuesday with nothing to post is still a real day. A hard season nobody documented still happened, and still shaped you, whether or not it ever appeared anywhere. If the only life that counts is the one that gets witnessed, an enormous amount of an actual life quietly gets treated as though it never occurred at all.

Who You Are Without the Audience

Here is a genuinely useful question, and it is worth answering honestly rather than quickly. If the platform disappeared tomorrow, every account gone, no more posting, no more audience of any size, what part of how you currently live would change.

For some people, very little would change, and that is a good sign, evidence that the sharing has stayed in its proper place, a pleasant extra rather than a load bearing wall. For others, the honest answer is considerably more, and that answer is not a failure. It is simply useful information about how much weight a curated self has quietly been asked to carry.

What Sharing Was Always Meant to Be

None of this is an argument against sharing your life. Documenting real joy, staying connected to people far away, building something creative in public, these are genuinely good uses of the same tools that can just as easily become a burden. The difference was never really the platform. It is whether the sharing is an overflow of a life you are actually living, or a substitute performance standing in for one you have quietly stopped fully inhabiting.

There is a simple test worth applying here, the same kind this book has offered for other identities built to survive something. Notice whether posting comes before or after the moment actually mattered to you. If you enjoyed the dinner first, and photographed it second, almost as an afterthought, the sharing is doing what it was always meant to do. If part of you was arranging the table with the photograph already in mind, the order has quietly reversed, and it is worth asking, without judgment, when that reversal happened and what it has been costing you since.

A life does not require witnesses in order to have mattered. That was true long before any of this technology existed, and it remains true now, on the ordinary Tuesdays nobody photographs, in exactly the same way it was true on the boat, in the light, two summers ago.

✦

SOUL MIRROR

If nobody could see it, would you still be living this particular version of your life?

TIMELESS WISDOM

A curated life can be a true reflection of a real one. It becomes something else the moment it stops reflecting your life and starts replacing it.

RENEWAL PRACTICE: The Unposted Life

For one week, keep a private list, seen by no one, of the moments you would normally consider posting. Do not post them. Simply write down what happened and how it actually felt, including the parts that would never have made the caption.

At the end of the week, read the list back. Notice how much of what mattered most to you that week never would have made it online at all, and let that list stand as its own quiet evidence of a life that does not require an audience in order to be real.

CHAPTER TEN

The Need to Belong

✦

BY HIS FOURTH month at the new job, he had noticed something he could not quite place at first.

He was good at the work. The team liked him, or seemed to, and he had settled into the easy rhythm of an office that jokes a certain way, takes lunch a certain way, talks about the weekend a certain way. He fit. It had taken effort in the beginning, learning the rhythm, but it no longer felt like effort. It felt like simply how he was.

Then one evening, describing his week to an old friend from college, he mentioned a hobby he used to talk about constantly and had not brought up once at the new job, not because anyone had ever discouraged it, but because it did not quite fit the version of himself the office had come to know. His friend asked him a simple question. *Do you still even do that anymore?* He realized, mid answer, that he did, most weekends, and that he could not remember the last time he had mentioned it to a single person he worked with.

Nothing dramatic had happened. Nobody had asked him to hide it. He had simply, quietly, without ever deciding to, stopped bringing pieces of himself into a room that had never actually rejected them, because it was easier not to test whether they belonged there.

A Need, Not a Weakness

Wanting to belong is not a flaw to be corrected. It is closer to a basic requirement, the same category as needing food or rest, and treating it as something to simply grow out of misunderstands what it actually is. Human beings were built for connection, for community, for a place where their name is known and their absence would actually be noticed. None of that is a character defect.

What this chapter is actually asking is narrower, and it matters. Is the belonging you have built on being known, or on being accepted. Those sound similar and are not the same thing at all.

THE PAIN OF BEING LEFT OUT

Think back to childhood for a moment. A birthday party you were not invited to. A group that would not let you join. A table where nobody thought to save you a seat. For a child, moments like these can feel enormous, entirely out of proportion to what an adult onlooker would consider a small social slight, and that is exactly right, because they are not really about the party. They are about a much larger question a child is asking for the first time. Do I belong.

Adults experience the exact same ache in more sophisticated packaging. A group chat you did not know existed. Coworkers who went somewhere without mentioning it. A family decision made without you in the room. Sometimes it genuinely does not matter, and sometimes it does, and the difference is rarely about the size of the event. It is about whether the event touches that same old question, still waiting underneath most adults exactly where it was left in childhood.

BELONGING IS MORE THAN BEING PRESENT

You can be in a room and not feel that you belong there. You can be part of a family and still feel, most of the time, like a guest in it. You can attend the same community every week for a decade and never once feel fully known inside it. Presence and belonging are not the same thing, and it is worth being honest about which one you actually have in a given relationship.

Real belonging carries something more specific than simply being allowed in the room. It says, there is room here for me, not merely for what I provide, not only on the days I agree, not only when I am useful or impressive or convenient. For me, specifically, on the ordinary days too.

WHEN BELONGING COMES WITH CONDITIONS

Every healthy group has some standards, and that is not what this section is about. Families need basic respect. Workplaces need professionalism. Friendships need a measure of trust to function at all. None of that is the problem.

The problem arrives when belonging quietly becomes conditional on something considerably narrower, do not disagree, do not grow in a direction that makes anyone uncomfortable, do not become more successful than the room can tolerate, do not leave the role you were assigned years ago. At that point belonging has stopped being a place to be known and become a price paid in self-erasure, and the specific danger is that this shift almost never gets announced. It simply becomes the unwritten rule of the room, discovered slowly, usually the hard way.

FITTING IN AND BELONGING ARE DIFFERENT JOBS

Fitting in asks what a room requires and then quietly supplies it. Belonging asks something considerably harder, and considerably better. It asks whether you can bring your actual self into that room and still be wanted there.

The test is not whether you ever adjust your behavior. Everyone does that, and doing it is not automatically a problem. You speak differently in a client meeting than you do on the phone with your sister, and that is simply what it means to move through different parts of a life. The real question is whether you have to become a genuinely different person in order to feel safe somewhere, or whether you are still fundamentally reachable underneath the adjustment. Fitting in studies a room and performs accordingly. Belonging actually participates in it. The two can look identical for months at a time, right up until the room asks something of the version of you it has never actually met.

THE SMALL, CONSTANT EDITS

Self-editing rarely arrives as one dramatic decision. It shows up in inches, an opinion not voiced because it would complicate the mood, a preference kept quiet because nobody else in the group seems to share it, a piece of your history left out because it does not fit the story this particular room already has of you.

None of these edits feel significant individually, which is exactly why they accumulate so easily. A person can go an entire year making small, reasonable sounding adjustments and arrive on the other side of it having genuinely lost track of what they think when nobody else's preference is in the room to react to. This is not weakness. It is simply what happens when belonging quietly gets confused with sameness, and nobody along the way stopped to ask whether the confusion was necessary.

WHY IT STARTS SO YOUNG

Nobody teaches a child to do this on purpose. One child discovers that quiet keeps a room calm. Another discovers that humor earns friends fast. Another goes tough because softness gets mocked on the playground. Each of them is asking, underneath the adjustment, the same simple question. What version of me actually works here.

By adolescence the stakes feel enormous, and adjustments can happen at real speed, a change of clothing, of interests, of who a person claims to admire, entirely in service of a group whose actual approval was never guaranteed to begin with. What makes adolescence so intense is not only the desire to belong, which every person carries, but the sheer number of untested assumptions running the whole operation. Almost nothing has actually been risked yet. Almost every belief about which version of yourself a group will accept is still a guess dressed up as certainty, and a great deal of the teenage years gets spent defending that guess as though it were already proven fact.

Adults do the same thing with better production values. We buy things partly for what they signal. We keep an opinion quiet in a room where it might land badly. The surroundings changed considerably since fifteen. The underlying need to be let in did not change at all.

TWO ROOMS, TWO VERSIONS

She moved to a new country at twenty six for work, and within a few years had built a genuinely good life there, close friends, a career she liked, a rhythm to her weeks that felt entirely her own. She also noticed, without ever quite deciding it consciously, that she had become two slightly different people depending on which room she was in.

With her new friends, she was easygoing, quick with a certain kind of dry humor that landed well at dinner parties, comfortable letting silences sit. On video calls home to her family, something in her posture changed before she had even said a word, a warmth that came more readily, a deference to her parents' opinions that she did not extend nearly as automatically to anyone in her new city. Neither version was fake. Both were simply what each room, over years, had quietly come to expect of her, and she had supplied it, the way most people supply whatever a room seems to want, without ever formally agreeing to the arrangement.

What unsettled her, when she finally noticed it, was not that the two versions existed. It was that she genuinely could not say, with any confidence, which one was closer to who she actually was when nobody was asking anything of her at all. She had spent so long being fluent in what each room required that the version of her underneath both had gone quiet from disuse, not erased, exactly, but definitely out of practice.

What Belonging Actually Requires

Real belonging asks more of a room than fitting in does, and it asks more of you as well. It requires being known, not merely accepted, which means it requires occasionally testing whether the people around you can handle an honest answer, a genuine opinion, a piece of you that does not match the room's existing picture. That is a risk. Fitting in was always the safer choice precisely because it never required that particular risk to be taken.

But safety of that kind has its own cost, paid slowly. A person who has spent years being accepted everywhere and known almost nowhere can eventually find themselves surrounded by people and still fundamentally alone in every room they enter, because nobody in any of those rooms has actually met them. This is its own quiet kind of loneliness, distinct from simple isolation, since it can exist right in the middle of a full social calendar. Everyone likes the version of you they were shown. That is real, and it is also not quite the same thing as being known, and the gap between the two can ache in a way that is hard to explain to anyone, including yourself.

Healthy Difference Does Not End Belonging

One sign of a genuinely secure sense of belonging is that disagreement does not immediately feel like danger. You can hold a different opinion than the group and remain part of it. You can decline an invitation without the friendship visibly cooling. You can say a true thing that lands a little awkwardly and watch the room absorb it and move on, rather than watching it quietly reorganize around your absence.

This is worth testing deliberately rather than simply hoping it turns out to be true. Most people never actually run the test. They assume, based on a handful of small early signals, sometimes accurate and sometimes not, that a given room requires agreement, and they organize years of behavior around an assumption that was never actually confirmed. If belonging only survives total agreement, it was never really belonging. It was closer to membership in something conditional, renewed constantly through continued sameness, and that kind of arrangement asks something from a person that real connection never should.

NOT EVERY ROOM IS YOURS

This part is harder to accept than it sounds. There are rooms where you simply will not fit, groups whose values run differently than yours, professional spaces where you are not selected, friendships that never quite deepen no matter how much good will both people bring to them. This does not always mean someone did something wrong. Sometimes two people, or a person and a group, simply do not connect, for reasons that have nothing to do with either party's worth.

You do not have to belong everywhere, and that realization, properly absorbed, can bring real freedom. Some closed doors are not rejection. They are simply direction, pointing you, often more efficiently than you would have found on your own, toward the rooms that were actually built to hold you.

WHAT BELONGING SHOULD NEVER COST

It is worth asking plainly, every so often, what you have had to set down in order to remain accepted somewhere. Your honest opinion. A boundary you needed. A piece of what you actually want out of life. If belonging repeatedly requires you to trade away something essential, the price has quietly become too high, whatever the room happens to be. Belonging was always meant to connect you to people. It was never meant to be the mechanism that slowly erases you in front of them.

A FEW THREADS WORTH NAMING AND SETTING ASIDE

Several other shapes of this same need deserve real attention and are getting it, just not here. A fear that people will eventually leave, rooted in an earlier loss, can make ordinary silences feel dangerous and ordinary space feel like rejection. That thread runs deep enough to need its own room later in this series. Being chosen by one particular person can quietly become the whole proof of your worth, so completely that its absence feels unbearable. That gets its own full chapter shortly. And learning to belong fully to yourself, before you can belong well to anyone else, is important enough that this book saves an entire chapter for it near the very end. Consider all three noted, and worth returning to when their turn comes.

When Growth Changes the Room

Sometimes belonging shifts not because anything went wrong, but because you changed. A promotion, a move, a season of real healing, and suddenly some old relationships do not fit quite the way they used to, while the new ones have not yet had time to feel like home either. That in between space is genuinely uncomfortable, and it is worth naming as its own thing rather than mistaking it for failure. You are not required to keep every relationship exactly as it was in order to prove you have not changed for the worse. Sometimes healing itself is what makes an old shared language, built around complaint or crisis or chaos, stop fitting the person you are becoming, and that transition can feel lonely for a while before it feels like anything else. The space is not evidence that something has gone wrong. It is usually evidence that something already has gone right, and the rest of your life simply has not caught up to it yet.

You Still Need People

None of this is an argument for needing nobody. Identity work sometimes tips a person toward a kind of proud self-sufficiency that sounds like health and is actually just a quieter version of the same old fear, dressed as independence instead of compliance. That is not the destination this chapter has in mind.

What actually changes is not the need for people, which never goes away and was never supposed to. What changes is what you are asking them for. Not *complete me,* but *know me.* Not *tell me whether I matter,* but *share an honest life alongside me.* You are allowed to need people. You are simply no longer required to let their opinion of you double as the only mirror you own.

WHAT THEY DID WITH IT

The man from the beginning of this chapter did not quit his job or announce a dramatic reinvention at the next team meeting. He simply mentioned the hobby, offhand, the following week, in a conversation that had nothing to do with it. A colleague, mildly surprised, asked a genuine question about it. Nothing fell apart. Nobody looked at him differently. It had never actually been forbidden. He had simply never tested whether the room could hold it, and the test, once finally run, turned out to cost him almost nothing.

She did something quieter still. On her next call home, in the middle of an ordinary conversation, she let herself disagree with her mother about something small, gently, without the usual deference arriving first to soften it. Her mother pushed back briefly, then let it go, and the call ended the way it always did, warmly, nothing broken. It was such a small moment that she almost didn't notice it had happened at all, and that was exactly the point. The room had never actually required the version of her that showed up automatically. She had simply never checked.

Not every room will pass that test. Some genuinely cannot hold the honest version of you, and that is real information worth having, not a failure on your part. But a room never tested can never actually be trusted either way, and a great many people spend years assuming rejection from rooms that were simply never given the chance to surprise them.

✦

SOUL MIRROR

Where do you feel you must perform in order to remain accepted, and what version of yourself shows up there instead of you?

TIMELESS WISDOM

Healthy belonging does not require you to disappear. You can love deeply without losing yourself, belong somewhere without agreeing with everything in it, and need people without asking them to tell you who you are.

RENEWAL PRACTICE: The Editing Log

For three days, notice every time you hold something back, an opinion, a preference, a piece of your history, in order to remain comfortable in a room. Write down what you held back and where.

At the end of the three days, sort the list into two piles. The first is simple courtesy, the ordinary discretion everyone reasonably practices. The second is concealment, things you did not say because you genuinely doubted the room could hold them.

The first pile is maturity. The second pile is the actual cost of that particular room, and it is worth knowing the number before you decide whether the room is worth the price.

CHAPTER ELEVEN

When Culture Tells You Who to Be

✦

SHE CAUGHT THE bouquet at her cousin's wedding entirely by accident, more or less falling into her hands as she stepped back to avoid the crush of women near the dance floor, and she was still holding it, slightly bewildered, when the first *you're next!* arrived from a table of aunts who meant it warmly.

By the end of the reception she had heard some version of it perhaps a dozen times. From the aunts. From her cousin's new mother in law. From a family friend who had known her since she was six and clearly meant it as the kindest thing she could think to say. She smiled and thanked each of them and drove home a little after midnight turning a question over that had not troubled her in months.

She was thirty six, established in a career she had built carefully and actually liked, living in an apartment she had chosen and furnished exactly to her own taste, genuinely content most days in a way she did not take for granted. None of that had changed in the four hours she spent at that wedding. But somewhere between the ceremony and the drive home, a life she quietly enjoyed had started to feel, for the first time in a long while, like a delay.

THE SCRIPT NOBODY HANDED YOU DIRECTLY

Culture gives everyone a script, and it does this so early and so consistently that most people absorb it the way they absorb a native language, without ever experiencing it as instruction. Marry by a certain point. Have children by a certain point, and a certain number of them. Reach a certain career milestone by a certain age. The script varies by community, by generation, by faith background, by country, but the mechanism underneath it is remarkably consistent everywhere it shows up. A timetable exists, largely unspoken, and falling behind it feels like a verdict rather than simply a different pace.

We already touched on something like this earlier in this book, both in how families quietly hand down expectations and in how a whole community can decide who a person is supposed to become before that person has had any real say in the matter. This chapter is where that thread gets its full attention, because culture is bigger than any one family, and its script reaches into rooms a family never even enters.

WHAT CULTURE GIVES US HONESTLY

Before going further, it is worth saying plainly that culture is not the villain of this chapter. A shared culture gives people something genuinely valuable, continuity, a sense of belonging that spans generations, an inherited set of values that did not need to be invented from nothing. Traditions carry real wisdom, tested across more years than any single life could test anything on its own. None of this chapter is arguing for treating your culture as an enemy to be escaped.

Think of everything a strong culture hands a person without their ever having to earn it. A ready made community at every wedding, every funeral, every ordinary Sunday. A set of holidays that already know how to be celebrated, recipes and rituals that do not need to be invented from scratch. A working answer, however imperfect, to enormous questions like how to raise a child or grieve a loss or grow old with some dignity. People who reject an entire cultural inheritance in one motion, out of frustration with one or two of its expectations, often find themselves rebuilding all of that scaffolding alone, slowly, at real cost, and are sometimes surprised by how much they actually miss it.

What is worth examining is narrower, and more useful. Not whether culture matters, but which of its specific expectations you have actually chosen, and which ones you have simply been carrying without ever once setting them down to look at them clearly.

THE TIMETABLE AND WHAT IT COSTS

The social clock, the general sense of what should have happened by what age, is one of culture's most powerful exports, and it operates almost entirely through comparison with people who are, on paper, exactly like you. Your college roommate is engaged. Your younger cousin already has two children. A former classmate just made partner, and you have not yet, and the timetable does not actually ask whether your own life circumstances, priorities, or path bear any resemblance to theirs. It simply notices the gap and asks you to feel behind because of it.

The strange thing about the social clock is how little it actually knows about the person it is judging. It has no information about your particular resources, your health history, the specific opportunities that were or were not available to you, the years spent caring for someone else that never show up on any timeline anyone compares you against. It only knows the calendar, and it applies the same generic schedule to every life it touches, regardless of how different those lives actually are underneath.

Falling short of a cultural timetable can produce real grief, and that grief deserves honesty rather than dismissal. But an unmet timeline is not the same thing as a wasted life, and the shame that timelines produce is frequently disproportionate to anything that has actually gone wrong.

DIFFERENT EXPECTATIONS, SAME WEIGHT

Culture does not distribute its scripts evenly. What is expected of a man in a given community often looks different from what is expected of a woman in that same community, and both scripts can carry real weight even when they point in entirely different directions. A man may feel pressure to be the provider, the strong one, the one whose worth is measured largely by career and income. A woman may feel pressure toward marriage and motherhood on a specific timeline, regardless of what she has actually built or hopes to build instead. Neither script is inherently wrong to want. The trouble starts when a person has never actually examined whether they want it, or have simply always assumed they must, because the assumption arrived so early it never felt like a choice at all.

He found this out directly when his wife's job offer came through, a genuinely better opportunity than anything either of them had on the table, in a city two states away, and the honest math of their household pointed clearly toward him staying home with their two young kids while she took it. He wanted to. That was the part that surprised him most, once he sat with it, how much he actually wanted the version of life that was being offered rather than merely tolerating it for practicality's sake.

Explaining it to his father was harder than making the actual decision had been. Not because his father said anything cruel. He didn't. But there was a pause on the phone, a beat too long, and then a question that was really a whole worldview compressed into six words. *So what will you tell people?* His father had spent forty years being exactly the kind of provider the question assumed was the only real option, and had built a great deal of his own worth on doing it well. The question was not really about what to tell people. It was about whether the script that had organized an entire life still had room in it for a son who was choosing something else.

He told people the truth, in the end, plainly, and most of them adjusted faster than he expected. A few never quite did. That turned out to be survivable in a way the original phone call had not made it feel like it would be.

This book is not going to tell you which parts of your particular cultural inheritance to keep and which to release. That decision belongs to you, and it deserves more care than any book written for a broad audience could responsibly offer on your behalf. What this chapter can do is help you notice, clearly, which expectations are actually operating on you, so the choice, whatever it turns out to be, is at least a real one.

TESTING WHETHER A VALUE IS ACTUALLY YOURS

Here is a useful, if uncomfortable, test. Take something you currently believe a good life must include, and ask whether you can defend it in writing without once mentioning what anyone else would think of you for having it or not having it.

If the defense holds up entirely on its own, that value is very likely genuinely yours, chosen or at least examined rather than simply inherited, and worth keeping exactly as it is. If the only defense you can produce leans on other people's opinions, *because that's just what people do,* or *because my family would be devastated otherwise,* that does not necessarily mean the value is wrong. It means it has not actually been tested yet, and an untested value is not the same thing as a chosen one, even when it happens to be correct.

WHAT HAPPENED AT THE WEDDING

The woman with the bouquet did not come home from that reception and reject marriage, or her family, or the wedding itself, which had genuinely been a lovely day. What she did, over the following weeks, was something quieter. She asked herself honestly whether the life she was building, the one that had felt entirely sufficient until a room full of well meaning relatives suggested otherwise, was actually missing something she wanted, or whether it had simply been measured, for one evening, against a schedule that was never actually hers to keep.

She concluded, after real thought, that she did want marriage eventually, genuinely, not merely because a schedule demanded it. That mattered. The wanting was hers now, examined and kept, rather than simply absorbed and obeyed. The bouquet sat on her kitchen counter for a week afterward, and then she threw it away, not as a rejection of anything, but because it had finished doing its job. It had asked her a question worth answering honestly, and she finally had.

✦

SOUL MIRROR

Which of your current goals would survive if the people you are trying to satisfy never found out whether you had reached them?

TIMELESS WISDOM

Culture can hand you a timetable, but it was never actually qualified to write your particular life. You are allowed to keep what still fits and release what was only ever borrowed.

RENEWAL PRACTICE: Given or Chosen

List eight beliefs you currently hold about what a good life must include. For each one, mark it *given* or *chosen.*

Then pick three and defend each one in writing without mentioning anyone else's expectations, approval, or opinion at any point in the defense.

Whatever cannot be defended this way is not disqualified. It simply has not been examined yet, and examining it, honestly, is the whole of what this chapter is asking you to do.

CHAPTER TWELVE

The Performing Self

✦

THE FIRST REAL vacation in six years, and she spent the second morning of it sitting by the pool with her laptop closed, physically present, doing absolutely nothing, and finding the nothing almost unbearable.

Not because she was bored. Because some part of her kept quietly cataloging everything the stillness meant she was not doing. Three unread emails she knew about without checking. A proposal that could be further along. The particular restlessness of a body trained for fifteen years to treat motion as proof of its own worth, suddenly asked to simply exist by a pool for a week, and not entirely sure how.

By the third day she caught herself thinking a sentence she had thought a hundred times before without ever really hearing it. *I'll actually relax once this next thing is finished.* She was on vacation. There was no next thing, not this week. And still the sentence arrived anyway, out of habit, looking for a task to attach itself to.

There is nothing wrong with wanting to succeed, with ambition, or with the genuine satisfaction of finishing something difficult. This chapter is not going to ask you to want less. It is going to ask a narrower question. Somewhere along the way, for people like the woman by the pool, achievement stopped being something pursued and started being something needed, and there is a real difference between the two.

Doing Well and Being Well Are Not the Same Thing

Picture two people working toward an identical goal, equally disciplined, equally likely to succeed. One thinks, *I want to do this well because it matters to me.* The other thinks, *I have to do this well, because I don't know who I am if I fail.*

From the outside, they are indistinguishable. Inside, one of them is pursuing excellence and the other is defending an identity. One can experience failure as disappointment. The other experiences it as exposure. That difference rarely shows up on a résumé, but it shows up everywhere else, in how each of them sleeps the night before a big decision, and in how each of them talks about the thing that didn't work out.

The Applause That Fades Faster Than Expected

Achievement produces a genuinely wonderful feeling, and the feeling reliably does not last as long as anyone expects it to. The degree goes into a frame. The new office becomes just your office. The milestone becomes a line on a biography, and another goal quietly takes its place on the horizon.

None of that is a flaw in you. It is simply what happens when satisfaction is asked to do a job it was never built for. Success can produce real satisfaction. It cannot permanently supply identity, and the gap between what it gives and what gets asked of it is where a great deal of quiet exhaustion comes from.

The Finish Line That Keeps Moving

I'll finally feel accomplished once I finish this. You finish it. *Maybe once I get the promotion.* You get it. Then somebody earns more, or achieves it younger, or does it more visibly, and there is a new number waiting on the other side of the old one.

This is why people who are, by any outside measure, remarkably successful can still privately feel as though they have never quite done enough. The problem is rarely a lack of achievement. It is that achievement has been handed a job, proving worth, that it structurally cannot finish, because worth was never something that could be proved through accumulation in the first place.

WHY REST FEELS LIKE GUILT

I'll rest when this project is done. When the kids are older. When things settle down. Then that season ends and another one starts, and rest keeps getting rescheduled into a future that never quite arrives, the way it did for the woman by the pool with nothing left to finish and no idea how to simply stop anyway.

For some people, this is not really about time at all. Stillness removes the familiar signal that tells them they are useful, responsible, worth having around, and the silence that follows can raise an uncomfortable question almost immediately. If I am not producing anything right now, am I wasting this. That question, however briefly it surfaces, reveals something considerably deeper than a full calendar.

Some people rest physically while remaining fully at work emotionally, watching a movie while running a mental list, on vacation while checking email every hour. Nothing ever feels completely finished, and because nothing feels finished, rest never quite feels earned either. But if rest has to be earned first, there is always going to be one more task standing between you and permission to stop.

THE CHILD WHO LEARNED THAT DOING WELL WAS SAFE

For a great many people, achievement and worth got wired together early. A good grade brought real warmth. A disappointing one brought something colder. Nobody necessarily said the sentence out loud, *you are only valuable when you succeed,* but a child pays close attention to which version of themselves gets the warmest reception, and adjusts accordingly.

This can build genuine strengths, real discipline, real focus, and those are not to be dismissed. But underneath the discipline, there is sometimes still a frightened child quietly making sure nobody becomes disappointed again. The classroom disappears by adulthood. The grades simply become a salary, a title, a follower count. The mechanism generating the fear never actually got the memo that school ended.

The Accomplished Person Who Feels Like a Fraud

Some genuinely accomplished people privately believe, with real conviction, that they do not deserve what they have built. Where others see competence, they see luck. Where others see expertise, they see only the enormous list of things they still do not know. Every compliment produces temporary relief and then evaporates, because the belief underneath it, *maybe I am not actually good enough,* was never actually addressed by the compliment in the first place.

So the person keeps collecting evidence. Another degree. Another success. But no amount of evidence ever quite closes the case, because the problem was never really the résumé. It was the belief standing behind it, and a belief does not get out-argued by more accomplishment. It gets examined directly, or it simply keeps absorbing whatever gets thrown at it and asking for more.

When Failure Stops Feeling Like an Event

Failure hurts everyone, and this chapter is not going to pretend otherwise. But when achievement has quietly become identity, failure stops being an event and starts being a verdict. *The business failed* becomes *I am a failure. The application was rejected* becomes *I am not good enough.*

At that point a person is no longer simply grieving an outcome. They are defending their entire sense of self, and that is why some people hide failures, minimize them, or become disproportionately crushed by a setback that a bystander would consider entirely survivable. The failure touched something the person had never realized was so exposed.

WHEN GOOD IS NEVER QUITE GOOD ENOUGH

Perfectionism looks like excellence from a distance, and up close the two are not the same thing at all. Excellence asks how something can be done well. Perfectionism asks how to make sure nobody can find anything wrong with it, and that is a considerably more frightened question wearing a much more respectable outfit.

Excellence can finish something and move on. Perfectionism keeps adjusting. Excellence can receive feedback as useful information. Perfectionism tends to experience feedback as a verdict, however gently it was delivered. A perfectionist can produce genuinely beautiful work and still walk away from it feeling nothing but its flaws, because perfectionism was never really scanning for evidence of success in the first place. It was scanning for evidence of inadequacy, and it will always find some, because that is what it was built to do.

This is also why perfectionism so often produces the opposite of productivity. If a thing must be done excellently, simply beginning becomes frightening, so the person researches, plans, and waits for a right moment that never quite arrives, then quietly criticizes themselves afterward for procrastinating. It rarely is laziness. It is usually fear, dressed comfortably enough that nobody, including the person wearing it, immediately recognizes it for what it is.

WHEN ACHIEVEMENT STARTS TO FUNCTION LIKE A DRUG

Achievement can create its own reward cycle. You accomplish something, people notice, you feel significant, and then the feeling fades and something in you goes looking for the next thing that will produce it again. The person caught in this cycle is often remarkably productive and widely admired for their drive, and privately never feels settled for more than a few days at a stretch. They are not only moving toward something anymore. They are also, quietly, running from the fear of becoming unremarkable, and those two motivations can look identical from the outside while feeling completely different on the inside.

A full calendar can start doing similar work, becoming its own kind of proof. An empty afternoon can feel oddly uncomfortable, so it gets filled, meeting after meeting, until exhaustion itself starts functioning as evidence that a life matters. But being constantly needed was never actually the same thing as being valuable, and a completely full life is not automatically evidence that it is being lived well.

When You Cannot Simply Receive Good News

Achievement-based identity often has real trouble celebrating anything. Someone says, *this is wonderful,* and the immediate internal response is a list of everything that could have gone better. There is real humility, and then there is something else entirely, an inability to let anything good simply land. They are not the same, and constantly diminishing your own work is not automatically a form of modesty. Sometimes it is simply evidence that the internal standard in charge has never once allowed satisfaction to be the final word.

A Brief Word on What Comes Later

Two threads worth naming here deserve more room than this chapter alone can give them. One is what happens when success itself changes how people treat you, and losing that treatment starts to feel like losing your worth along with it. The other, closely related, is what happens on the specific day a title disappears, at retirement, after a business is sold, when the office is somebody else's now. Both of those get a full chapter of their own further ahead in this book, because each deserves a complete telling rather than a paragraph here.

YOUR GIFT IS NOT THE SAME THING AS YOUR WORTH

You may be genuinely, unusually gifted at something. That is worth developing and worth celebrating honestly, without false modesty standing in the way. But a gift is something you possess. It was never meant to be the measure of your value as a person. This distinction protects two things at once, your confidence and your humility, because you do not have to pretend to be less capable than you are, and you also do not have to believe that being exceptional at something makes you more human than someone whose gifts simply draw less attention.

WHAT ACHIEVEMENT LOOKS LIKE WITHOUT THE FEAR UNDERNEATH IT

Healthy achievement still works hard, still sets real goals, still wants excellence, and still celebrates success honestly when it arrives. What changes is the foundation underneath it. Instead of *I must succeed to prove I matter,* it becomes *because my life already matters, I want to use it well.* Instead of *failure proves I am inadequate,* it becomes *failure gives me information about what happened.* Instead of needing to outperform everyone in the room, it simply asks whether you are still growing. This kind of ambition can move just as fast as the fear driven version. It simply is not being chased the entire way.

WHAT ACHIEVEMENT WAS NEVER MEANT TO PROVE

There is an old order worth remembering here, easy to miss because it runs against how most of us were actually raised to think. Worth was never meant to be something manufactured through endless performance. A life has value before the résumé exists, before the first achievement is ever recorded, and that changes the direction the whole chapter has been pointing toward. You do not work for your worth. You work from it. You are not required to achieve enough to earn permission to matter, and that is not an argument for doing less. It is a considerably stronger reason to do it well, because the work is now an expression of a life that already counted, rather than the price being paid for one.

WHAT YOU WOULD STILL DO

Here is a question worth sitting with honestly. If nobody could applaud you for it, what would you still want to do. What would you still create, still learn, still build, still show up for, even in a room with nobody watching.

Some answers will surprise you. You may discover you genuinely love the work itself, entirely apart from what it earns you, and that is a real and wonderful thing to find out. You may also notice that some of what you have been chasing was never really about the work at all. Neither discovery needs to be met with self judgment. Simply notice it, and then ask the question this whole chapter has been circling. What would it look like to pursue real excellence without needing that excellence to prove anything about your worth.

That question, sat with honestly, is where the freedom in this chapter actually begins.

✦

SOUL MIRROR

How comfortable are you with rest while there is still work you could be doing, and what thought shows up in you the moment you actually stop?

TIMELESS WISDOM

Achievement is a wonderful servant and a poor source of identity. Build, create, and work with everything you have. Just do not ask achievement to tell you whether your life matters. It was never built to carry that particular weight.

RENEWAL PRACTICE: Being and Doing

Draw two columns on a page.

In the first, list what you do. Lead a team. Raise a family. Run a business. Solve problems. Be as specific and complete as you like.

In the second, list who you are underneath those things, using character rather than job titles. Thoughtful. Curious. Compassionate. Still learning. Capable of real growth.

Look at which column has received most of your attention over the last several years. Then ask yourself honestly, if your ability to do any of the first column changed tomorrow, whether you would still know how to value the person listed in the second.

Finish by writing one sentence, and let it stand as it is.

My achievements are part of my story. They are not the measure of my worth.

CHAPTER THIRTEEN

The Faithful Self

✦

EVERYONE AT CHURCH called her a prayer warrior, and she was, genuinely, the kind of person other people called at midnight when something fell apart, because she always answered, and she always knew exactly what to say.

She led the women's ministry. She had discipled a dozen younger women through their own hardest years, sat with three different families through funerals, organized the meal train nobody else remembered to start. When her own marriage began quietly failing, she told almost no one, and the two people she did tell got a version of it wrapped so carefully in the right language that neither of them realized how bad it actually was.

We're just in a season. God is teaching us something. I have peace about it.

She did have peace, in the sense that the sentence was not entirely invented. But underneath the peace was something closer to terror, and she could not find a way to say the terror out loud in a room that had known her for eleven years as the strong one, the steady one, the woman whose faith never seemed to wobble. Admitting she was afraid felt, absurdly, like it would cost her something more than the marriage already was.

When Serving Started to Become Proving

There is nothing in this chapter that argues against genuine faith, real service, or a life spent caring for the people around you in the name of something larger than yourself. Those things are good, and for a great many people they are the most meaningful parts of an entire life. This chapter is asking a narrower, more specific question, the same one this book has asked about achievement and strength and being needed. Somewhere along the way, did serving stop being an overflow of what you believe, and start being the way you prove you belong.

The shift is quiet, and it usually starts with genuine gifting. Someone is good at leading, good at showing up, good at praying for people in ways that actually help, and the community responds warmly, as it should. But warmth repeated often enough can start to feel less like appreciation and more like a role that must now be maintained, and a person can wake up one day having quietly agreed to be the faithful one in every room they enter, without ever consciously signing up for the position.

This particular trap is harder to notice than most of the others in this book, precisely because everything about it looks like virtue from every angle. Nobody warns a devoted volunteer that devotion can quietly curdle into identity. The community keeps saying thank you, and meaning it, and the devoted person keeps showing up, and meaning that too, right up until showing up stops being a choice and starts being the only thing standing between them and the fear of becoming ordinary in a room that has only ever known them as exceptional.

THE SPIRITUAL MASK

Faith gives people a vocabulary, and most of that vocabulary is genuinely useful. But the same words that can carry real comfort can also become a way of avoiding honest emotion entirely, and it is worth learning to tell the two apart.

I'm blessed, said instead of *I'm struggling. I have peace about it,* said instead of *I am frightened and do not know what happens next. I'm trusting God,* said instead of *I have absolutely no idea what to do.* None of these phrases are lies, exactly. Most of the time they are half true, a real hope sitting right alongside a real fear, and only the hope gets spoken out loud. But truth and faith were never actually enemies. You can believe something is ultimately going to be all right and still be exhausted today. You can trust and still be afraid in the same breath. A spiritual vocabulary used to bypass honest feeling rather than carry it honestly is not evidence of strong faith. It is simply a more respectable looking mask than most.

The trouble with this particular mask is that it tends to get rewarded more consistently than almost any other kind. A person who says *I'm struggling* in most rooms gets a mixed response, real concern from some, mild discomfort from others, an awkward silence from a few who never quite know what to say next. A person who says *I'm trusting God through it* in a room full of believers usually gets warmth, admiration even, regardless of how true the sentence actually is underneath. That asymmetry teaches a lesson quickly, and it is a lesson worth naming plainly, because it means the most spiritually fluent people in any community can also become the ones least likely to ever say what is actually happening to them.

What Happens When You Cannot Serve

The real test of this pattern rarely shows up while everything is going well. It shows up the moment serving becomes impossible, through illness, through burnout, through a private failure that feels disqualifying, through a season of genuine doubt that nobody in the community would know what to do with if it were said out loud.

If your worth has quietly become tied to how faithfully you are seen to be serving, then the inability to serve does not simply feel like a scheduling problem. It feels like an identity crisis, sometimes even a spiritual one, when it was never actually meant to be either. A season of rest, doubt, or need was never evidence of a smaller faith. It is simply what being human occasionally requires, and a faith sturdy enough to be worth having should have room in it for exactly that.

DOUBT IS NOT THE OPPOSITE OF FAITH

For someone whose identity has become the reliably faithful one, honest doubt can feel like the single most dangerous thing to admit, more dangerous, often, than almost any other struggle this book has named. If faith is the entire foundation of how you are known, questioning it, even privately, even briefly, can feel like pulling out the one load bearing wall in the whole house.

But doubt and unbelief are not the same thing, and a faith that has never once been questioned is frequently a faith that has never actually been tested either. Many people who look back on a genuinely deep, resilient faith can point to a season where they were not sure of much at all, and came out the other side of it with something sturdier than what they carried in. The person who cannot admit to any doubt is not necessarily the person with the strongest faith. Sometimes they are simply the person most frightened of what the room would think if they were honest.

A DIFFERENT VERSION OF THE SAME WEIGHT

He had been a deacon for nine years, the kind of man younger guys in the church looked to without quite knowing why, steady, dependable, the one who prayed out loud without stumbling over the words. Nobody would have guessed that he had stopped believing, roughly, that any of it was true, somewhere around eighteen months earlier, in the aftermath of a diagnosis that had taken his younger brother in eleven weeks flat.

He kept showing up. Kept leading the Wednesday group, kept his hand raised during worship, kept saying the right things at the right moments, because the alternative, standing in front of people who had known him for a decade and admitting he was not sure he believed any of it anymore, felt considerably more frightening than simply continuing to perform a faith he no longer entirely felt. He told himself it would pass. Some weeks he almost believed that too.

What eventually moved him was not a sermon or a breakthrough. It was a conversation with an older man in the church, someone he had always assumed had it entirely figured out, who mentioned, offhand, over coffee, a two year stretch in his own life when he had barely believed anything at all and had kept showing up anyway, out of stubbornness more than conviction, waiting to see if the feeling would eventually catch up to the practice. It did, eventually, though not quickly, and not in a way he could have rushed.

That conversation did not fix anything immediately. But it did something almost as useful. It gave him one example, finally, of a faith that had survived genuine doubt without needing to pretend the doubt away, and it let him stop performing certainty he did not have, at least with that one person, at least for now.

What both of these stories share is not a resolution. Her marriage was still hard. His doubt did not vanish overnight simply because he finally said it out loud to one person. What changed, in both cases, was smaller and more durable than a resolution. Each of them found one person willing to meet the actual state of things rather than the performed version of it, and that single honest relationship did more for their faith, oddly enough, than years of looking flawless ever had.

Correction, Even Here

This book has spent real time on the difference between correction, which addresses something you did, and condemnation, which claims to name something you are. That distinction applies inside a faith community as much as anywhere else, and it is worth being honest about how easily the two get confused there specifically.

You have been distant lately, is everything all right is correction, offered with love, and it is worth being able to receive it. *A person with real faith wouldn't be struggling like this* is condemnation wearing spiritual language, and it does real damage regardless of who says it or how gently. The difference matters enormously here, because a community that only knows how to condemn a struggling faith will teach its most devoted people to hide exactly the parts of themselves that most need to be seen.

What Was Never Actually Required

The order worth remembering, the same one that has come up earlier in this book in different clothing, is that worth was never meant to be earned through visible devotion. A life already had value before the ministry began, before the ninetieth person was discipled, before a single prayer was ever said out loud in front of anyone. Service was always meant to be a response to that worth, not the price required to secure it.

This does not make service meaningless. It makes it considerably lighter to carry, because a person no longer has to perform faithfulness in order to remain acceptable. They are free to serve because they genuinely want to, and just as free to say, honestly, on the weeks it is true, that they are struggling, afraid, or simply tired, without any of it costing them their place.

She did eventually say the true version out loud, months later, to one woman in her small group she had known for years and trusted more than she had let herself admit. *I'm not okay. I haven't been for a while.* Nothing collapsed. The woman did not think less of her. If anything, something between them finally became real that had been performed for over a decade, and she found, to her genuine surprise, that being known honestly felt considerably more like faith than being admired ever had.

✦

Soul Mirror

If you could not serve, lead, or help anyone for an entire season, would you still believe you belonged in that community exactly as you are?

TIMELESS WISDOM

Faith was never meant to be a performance maintained for an audience. It was meant to be lived honestly, doubts and all, in front of people who love you enough to see the whole of it.

RENEWAL PRACTICE: The Honest Sentence

Think of one thing you have recently described using comfortable, faithful sounding language that was not the whole truth. *I'm blessed. I have peace about it. God's got this.*

Write the comfortable version first. Then write the honest sentence underneath it, the one you have not said out loud to anyone yet.

Choose one trusted person and say the honest version to them this week, even if the comfortable version remains true as well. Both can exist in the same sentence. Practice saying them together.

CHAPTER FOURTEEN

The Pleasing Self

✦

THE CALL CAME in at 11:40, the way it usually did, her sister's name on the screen, and she picked up before the second ring the way she always did, already reaching for a pen.

Twenty minutes of talking her sister through the crisis, mostly just listening, asking the right questions, helping her sister find her own way to a decision that was actually hers to make. It went well. It usually did. She hung up feeling the familiar, quiet satisfaction of having been useful to someone she loved.

Two days later her sister called again, cheerful this time, to say she'd handled the follow up herself, worked it out entirely on her own, hadn't even needed to think it through with anyone. Good news, plainly. She said so, meant it, was glad.

And underneath the gladness, so quietly she almost missed it, something else moved through her that she did not expect and did not much like once she noticed it. A small, unwelcome flicker of something close to loss. *She didn't need me for that one.*

The Person Everyone Calls

Every family seems to have one, and every friend group and every office has some version of the same person. The one who gets the 11:40 call. Financial trouble, call her. A decision that needs talking through, call him. Somebody is always the one everyone turns to, and often, genuinely, they are exactly the right person to turn to, capable, generous, willing to show up.

None of that is the problem this chapter is interested in. The problem is what happens quietly, over years, once being called on stops being simply something this person does and starts being the primary evidence they have that they matter at all.

Being Loved and Being Needed Are Not the Same Thing

This distinction is worth sitting with, because it is easy to feel and hard to say clearly. Someone can need you without actually knowing you. They may need your money, your advice, your steady presence in a crisis, your willingness to solve whatever has gone wrong, and every one of those needs can be entirely real without amounting to love in the fuller sense.

Healthy love appreciates what you give. It also, crucially, sees who you are on the days you have nothing left to give at all. A useful, uncomfortable question follows directly from this. If you stopped doing so much for a particular person, what would actually remain between the two of you. Sometimes the honest answer is a great deal. Sometimes the honest answer is considerably less than either person would like to admit.

When Someone Else's Strength Feels Like a Small Loss

Here is the part of this pattern that people rarely say out loud, mostly because it does not reflect well on anyone, even though it is remarkably common. You genuinely want the people you help to grow stronger. And some part of you, quietly, also wants to remain necessary to that strength once it arrives.

This is exactly what happened in the phone call at the start of this chapter. The sister solving her own problem was unambiguously good news. It was also, for one unwelcome moment, a small identity crisis, because if she no longer needed rescuing, a question opened up that had been comfortably closed for years. What is my place here now. If usefulness has been quietly doing the work of answering *do I matter*, then someone else's growing independence starts to feel, against every intention, like a small loss rather than the success it actually is.

WHEN USEFULNESS STARTS TO FEEL LIKE THE ONLY SAFETY

Why do some people give far past the point that is comfortable or even sustainable. Sometimes it really is simple generosity. But often, underneath the generosity, there is a quieter calculation running the whole time. If people need me, they will keep me. If I make myself indispensable, nobody actually leaves.

That fear rarely gets said aloud, even internally, but it explains a great deal of behavior that otherwise looks purely selfless. It can make someone else's growing independence feel like a genuine threat rather than the outcome you were supposedly working toward the entire time, and it is worth being honest with yourself about which of the two is actually driving a given act of generosity.

WHEN HELPING BECOMES A KIND OF CONTROL

This is uncomfortable to admit, and worth admitting anyway. Sometimes help crosses a line without anyone intending it to. Advice offered before it was requested. A problem fixed that the other person genuinely needed to learn to fix themselves. Money handed over repeatedly, with no responsibility attached, each time it happens again.

All of it can be called love, and sometimes it genuinely is. But sometimes it is fear wearing love's clothing, or something closer to control, quietly protecting your own necessary role in someone else's life rather than actually serving their growth. The harder, more useful question is not simply *am I helping*. It is *is my help actually making this person healthier, or is it protecting a pattern that keeps them, and me, exactly where we already are.*

A version of this shows up plainly around money. Someone repeatedly makes the same costly decision, and each time the crisis arrives, you cover it, relief follows, and nothing about the underlying pattern changes, because it never had to. Love sometimes helps. Love sometimes has to say no instead, and telling the two apart, in the moment, is genuinely difficult work rather than an easy formula.

THE YES THAT IS ACTUALLY RESENTMENT

Sure, no problem, said out loud, while something considerably less generous runs underneath it. *Why does it always have to be me.* That is not really a peaceful yes. It is a yes with resentment already loaded into it, and the other person usually has no idea, because from where they're standing, you simply said yes.

Resentment that shows up after helping is rarely proof the other person did something wrong. It is more often information about you, that you gave more than you actually wanted to give, that a boundary needed voicing and did not get voiced. This chapter cannot fully cover the work of building real boundaries, since a later chapter in this book is built specifically around exactly that. For now, it is enough to notice the resentment when it shows up, and to treat it as a signal worth listening to rather than a feeling to simply push past.

THE PARENT WHOSE CHILD GREW UP

Parenthood begins entirely built around being needed, a baby depends on you for nearly everything, and that is exactly as it should be at the start. The whole shape of good parenting, though, is a long, slow transfer away from that dependence, toward a child who increasingly does not need you in the same way, and that transition is harder for some parents than it has any right to be.

Advice keeps arriving after it stopped being requested. Decisions get quietly questioned. A grown child's independence starts to feel, unfairly, like distance or even rejection, when it is often simply proof that the earlier years of care actually worked. Love does not have to disappear as a child grows up. It has to change shape, and changing shape is not the same thing as being needed less.

Something similar shows up in leadership and in friendship, in a manager who cannot delegate because being indispensable feels like the whole of their value, or a friend whose relationships are built almost entirely around being the one who fixes things in a crisis, with very little room left over for the ordinary, uneventful enjoyment of each other's company. The shape changes. The underlying question does not. Am I needed for what I actually offer, or only for what I fix.

LETTING SOMEONE CARRY WHAT IS ACTUALLY THEIRS

One of the harder lessons for a person who has built real identity around helping is that not every burden you are capable of carrying is yours to carry. Someone else's disappointment can belong to them. Someone else's financial choices can belong to them. Someone else's conflict, someone else's consequences, can genuinely belong to them, and you are allowed to care deeply about a person without taking ownership of everything happening in their life.

There is a real middle ground between indifference and rescue, and it sounds something like *I am here with you,* without automatically becoming *I will fix this for you.* You can listen without solving. Support without controlling the outcome. That kind of presence respects both people in the relationship, rather than quietly asking one of them to disappear into usefulness.

WHEN SOMEONE ELSE'S PROBLEMS ARE EASIER THAN YOUR OWN

There is a quieter reason some people over-give that is worth naming honestly. Someone else's crisis is often considerably easier to face than your own unattended life. Their problem gives you somewhere concrete to direct your attention, and while you are directing it there, your own marriage, your own exhaustion, your own postponed plans, get to sit quietly untouched a while longer.

Helping others is genuinely good. It stops being good the moment it becomes the place you hide from the parts of your own life that actually need your attention.

You Are Valuable on the Day Nobody Calls

You already met a version of this question at the very start of this book, when everything you do for other people was stripped away on paper to see what remained. It is worth asking again here, more specifically. Imagine a day when nobody calls with a crisis. Nobody needs advice, or money, or rescuing. Nobody needs you to fix anything at all.

Who are you on that particular day. Still valuable. Still worth loving. If the honest answer feels uncertain, that uncertainty is not a character flaw. It is simply pointing at exactly where this chapter's real work is waiting.

What Service Was Always Meant to Be

There is an old and simple order worth remembering here. Real service flows from love that already exists. It was never meant to be the method by which love gets purchased or secured. One version says, *I serve because I genuinely care.* The other says, quietly underneath, *I serve so that you will need me enough to stay.* The two can look completely identical from the outside, the same phone picked up, the same help given. What differs entirely is whether the giver can also rest, or whether resting feels like a risk they cannot afford to take.

✦

SOUL MIRROR

Finish this honestly. If people did not need me, I am afraid ______.

TIMELESS WISDOM

Being needed can make you feel important. Being loved lets you remain important even on the days you have nothing left to give. Learn to want the second one more than the first.

RENEWAL PRACTICE: The Responsibility Test

Think of one person you regularly help, and answer four questions honestly on paper.

What actually belongs to you in this, listening, encouraging, reasonable support, a kept commitment.

What belongs entirely to them, their decisions, their effort, their consequences, their own growth.

What are you currently carrying that, if you are honest, actually belongs to them.

What would real support look like if you let go of controlling how it turns out.

Then write one sentence and leave it exactly as it is. I can love someone without taking responsibility for everything in their life.

CHAPTER FIFTEEN

The Successful Self

✦

FOR ELEVEN YEARS, he had imagined what it would feel like to reach this exact position.

The years had asked more of him than most people around him ever saw. There were late nights, interrupted vacations, difficult decisions made in rooms other people had avoided, and long stretches when progress seemed much slower than the effort required to produce it. He had watched colleagues move ahead of him more than once and wondered whether his own turn would come at all. Twice he had nearly left the company entirely. Both times he stayed because he believed he was building toward something specific, something that would eventually make the years of sacrifice feel complete.

Then, on an ordinary Tuesday morning, the promotion came.

By lunchtime his phone was full of congratulations. His wife booked the restaurant he liked best. His mother cried when he called her. Friends who had watched him work toward this for years told him how proud they were, and he was proud too, genuinely and with every right to be.

Within days, however, something he had not expected began to happen. The congratulations became less frequent. The impressive new office slowly became simply the place where he worked. One morning he sat behind the desk he had wanted for more than a decade, looked out at the view he had once imagined would feel like arrival, and realized that he felt strangely unchanged.

He had expected the promotion to settle an old question: whether he had done enough, whether he had finally reached the place where he could relax and know that his life counted for something. Instead, the title had changed, the office had changed, the number on his paycheck had changed, and the person sitting behind the desk was still carrying most of the same questions he had carried the week before.

For the first time, he began to wonder whether he had been asking success to give him something it was never actually built to provide.

WHEN SUCCESS TAKES ON A SECOND JOB

There is nothing wrong with wanting to succeed. Ambition, discipline, financial progress, education, leadership, and the satisfaction of building something difficult and watching it work can all be healthy parts of a full life. This chapter is not asking you to want less, lower your standards, or become suspicious of achievement.

The trouble begins when achievement quietly takes on a second responsibility. It is no longer simply something you have accomplished, it begins determining how you are allowed to feel about yourself.

There is a real difference between I want to succeed at this and the quieter, heavier belief, I need to succeed at this so I can feel that I matter. The first is a goal. The second has placed identity inside the outcome.

From the outside, the two people pursuing success may look almost identical. Both work hard. Both prepare. Both accept responsibility. Both may achieve remarkable things. The difference often becomes visible only when something goes wrong. One experiences failure as a painful result that needs to be understood. The other experiences failure as evidence about who they are. That is when success has stopped being only success. It has become a source of identity.

WHEN SUCCESS BEGAN AS AN ESCAPE PLAN

Not everyone who chases success this intensely is chasing applause. For some people, success began as an exit.

Perhaps you grew up watching money disappear before the month did. You saw what financial insecurity did to the adults around you. You remember unpaid bills, difficult choices, borrowed money, or the embarrassment of realizing that your family could not afford what other families seemed to take for granted. Somewhere in those years, a decision may have formed quietly. My life will be different.

That decision can build an extraordinary life, discipline, education, financial wisdom, resilience, opportunities that change not only your future but the future of people who come after you. There is real dignity in that kind of determination.

But survival has a strange habit of continuing after the danger that created it has passed. A person can become financially secure by any reasonable measure and still feel permanently unsafe. There is always another amount that would make things more certain, another qualification that would make the future safer. The circumstances changed. The alarm did not.

At some point the question has to change too. It can no longer stay can I build enough to escape where I came from. A more useful question becomes can I recognize that I am no longer there. Without that recognition, a person can spend the rest of life running from a place they left decades ago. The bank balance may belong entirely to the present while the fear still belongs to childhood.

SUCCESS AS AN ANSWER TO SOMEONE WHO HURT YOU

For other people, success runs on a different fuel entirely.

Someone said you would never amount to much. A teacher dismissed you. A parent repeatedly compared you with a sibling. A former partner made you feel small. You remembered, and somewhere inside, perhaps without ever consciously deciding it, success stopped being only about the life you wanted to build. It became an answer. I will show you.

This kind of motivation can produce remarkable results. Anger, humiliation, and the desire to prove someone wrong can generate enormous energy. But they are expensive fuels for an entire life. If your success is still quietly addressed to somebody who hurt you years ago, part of your life remains under their influence whether or not they know it, whether or not they even remember what they said. Their voice is still helping decide what you pursue, how hard you push, and what has to happen before you are finally allowed to feel vindicated.

Healing eventually asks an uncomfortable question. Do you want your future to remain a response to your past? You may continue building exactly the same things. The career can still matter. The reason simply gets to become yours, built because you love what you are building rather than because you are still trying to win an argument with someone who left the conversation years ago.

WHEN KEEPING IT BECOMES SCARIER THAN BUILDING IT

Success creates its own kind of pressure once it exists. Before you have something, the challenge is getting it. Afterward, the challenge becomes keeping it, a reputation to maintain, a lifestyle people have grown accustomed to, a standard that no longer feels optional.

The fear here is rarely about wanting more. It is about going backward, about what people might think if the house becomes smaller, the position changes, the company shrinks, or your name is no longer attached to the same level of influence. A person can remain in a career they no longer enjoy because leaving would look like decline. They can keep running a business at a size that consumes them because reducing it feels like admitting defeat. At that point success is no longer providing freedom. It is demanding maintenance, and it is worth asking honestly what all of it was actually for if it cannot eventually buy the freedom to decide how you want to live.

THE MORNING THE TITLE DISAPPEARED

Sometimes this entire pattern gets exposed gradually. Sometimes it happens on a single Monday morning.

Another man, thirty one years into a successful career, had a retirement party with a cake, a card everyone signed, and a thoughtful speech from the woman who would take over his position. He had planned the date financially for years. The pension was arranged. The mortgage was almost finished. He had even made a list of things he wanted to do once work no longer consumed most of the week.

What he had not prepared for arrived the following Monday. At nine fifteen he was sitting in his own kitchen with nowhere he was required to be. For more than three decades he had been introduced by a title so consistently that its presence had become invisible. It answered questions before they were asked. Now it was simply gone, and he sat looking at a calendar with almost nothing written on it, asking a question that felt, absurdly, brand new. Who am I now that nobody needs to know what I do?

Retirement did not create that question. It only turned off the machine that had been quietly answering it for thirty years. Who am I when my calendar is not full. Who am I when a younger person sits in the room where I once had the final word. Who am I when my experience is respected but no longer required every day. These are not small questions, and a career, however meaningful, was never designed to answer all of them.

WHEN POSSESSIONS BECOME EVIDENCE

Titles are not the only things people ask to carry their worth. Sometimes it is possessions, the house in the right neighborhood, the car in the driveway, the visible shape of a life that quietly communicates, things have gone well for me.

There is nothing wrong with enjoying the results of your work. A good home can bring genuine comfort. The issue is never the possession itself. It is the meaning quietly attached to it. If financial circumstances changed and you needed to live in a smaller house, would you experience that as a practical adjustment, or would some part of you feel that you had become smaller too? If you drove an older car after years of driving expensive ones, would the change touch your convenience, or your identity?

A house is somewhere you live. A car is something you drive. Neither one was ever issued as a report card on the worth of the person using it. Yet once success and identity become intertwined, downsizing starts to feel like humiliation and an ordinary financial setback starts to feel like a public confession. That is too much weight for a possession to carry.

WHEN SUCCESS BECOMES THE ONLY LANGUAGE YOU SPEAK

There is a subtler cost to years of building this way. Success can slowly become the main language a person knows how to relate to themselves in. They know how to set a goal, solve a problem, increase a number, measure progress. Ask what gives them joy that cannot be measured, and the answer comes slower. Ask what they enjoy that produces absolutely nothing, and it can come slower still.

Achievement trains a person to think in outcomes, which is genuinely useful in business and in a great many areas of life. But not everything worth having produces one. A conversation with your child does not need to advance anything. A slow dinner with a friend does not require a measurable return. Walking somewhere beautiful accomplishes nothing beyond the walk itself. A quiet afternoon with someone you love leaves no evidence behind except the memory of it. The successful self can genuinely struggle with moments like these, because they refuse to sit on any list of achievements. And yet these are so often exactly the moments people miss most once life changes. A life measured only by results will quietly overlook much of what made the results worth having in the first place.

THE COST NOBODY ADDS TO THE CALCULATION

Success always has a cost, and that is not, by itself, a warning. Anything worth building usually requires something real, time, effort, risk, sacrifice. The question worth asking is simply whether you know what you are actually paying.

A career may require several genuinely intense years. A business may demand unusual focus in its early seasons. These can be wise exchanges. But some people keep paying long after they have forgotten what they were originally trying to purchase. Another five years of absence from a family that needed them present. Another season of poor sleep. Another relationship quietly receiving only whatever energy happens to be left over after work has taken its share. Another promise to slow down next year, the way there was a promise the year before.

Success is not only what you gain. It is also what you exchange to gain it. This is not an argument for refusing to pay any price at all. It is an argument for knowing, plainly, what the price actually is, and deciding honestly whether what you are receiving in return still deserves it. A person can become genuinely successful at something that has quietly stopped deserving the amount of life being handed over for it.

REDEFINING WHAT SUCCESS EVEN MEANS

One of the more mature things a person can do, usually only after enough years to have earned it, is let their own definition of success actually change.

What counted as success at twenty five is rarely what should still count at fifty five. Early on it might mean establishing a career at all. Later it might mean having enough freedom left over to be genuinely present with the people you love. Early on it might mean increasing income. Later it might mean discovering how much less you actually need than you assumed. At one stage recognition matters enormously, because it is building credibility. Later, peace can matter considerably more than visibility. At one stage success might mean becoming indispensable. Later it might mean building something that runs well even on the days you are not in the room.

This is not a loss of ambition. It is frequently ambition finally growing up, and there is a real difference between climbing because there is still somewhere worth going and climbing because stopping would force you to face what the climbing has been covering.

PROUD WITHOUT NEEDING TO BE SUPERIOR

Some people worry that examining achievement this closely is an argument for false modesty. It is not. If you worked hard for something, say so. If you built something genuinely difficult, celebrate it without flinching. Pretending otherwise is not humility. It is simply a different kind of dishonesty.

You can say, plainly, I am very good at what I do, without that sentence needing a second half, and that makes me worth more than people who are not. Healthy identity does not require denying your strengths. It only asks that your strengths stop being the basis on which you decide your life outweighs someone else's.

COMING BACK TO THE WINDOW

He did not resign. There was no dramatic exit, no sudden decision that ambition had been meaningless all along. He genuinely liked the work, and once the strange flatness of that first week passed, he found real enjoyment in the responsibilities the promotion actually carried.

What changed was not the job. It was the job he had been asking the job to do inside him. He started protecting a few evenings instead of surrendering them automatically. He took a vacation without his laptop in the bag for the first time in years. He called a friend who had known him long before any of the titles and found it genuinely refreshing to spend an evening with someone who remained entirely unimpressed by his position. He started playing basketball again on

Saturday mornings, badly, which turned out to be most of the pleasure. Nothing to prove. Nothing to win except the game itself.

He began asking a different set of questions about the years ahead, ones that had nothing to do with what came next professionally. What kind of husband he wanted to be. Which friendships actually deserved more of his attention. How much money was genuinely enough. What parts of himself had gone almost entirely unattended because they could never advance a career. None of it made him less ambitious. It made the ambition considerably more intelligent, aimed at something sturdier than the next title.

Success stayed important to him. It simply stopped being asked to define the entire man, and that may be one of the healthier versions of success available to anyone: the point where what you have built becomes something you can genuinely enjoy, without ever again needing it to tell you who you are.

✦

SOUL MIRROR

What would success look like if you no longer needed it to prove that you matter?

TIMELESS WISDOM

Achievement can tell you a great deal about what you have done. It cannot give a final answer about what you are worth. You are more than the evidence of what you have accomplished.

RENEWAL PRACTICE: The Success Inventory

Divide a page into three columns.

In the first, list what you have actually achieved. Do not minimize it. Education, career progress, financial ground gained, a family raised, a hard season survived without becoming bitter.

In the second, write what you privately expected each achievement to finally prove. Safe. Respected. Equal to the people who doubted you. No longer ashamed of where you started. Write honestly, there is no wrong answer here.

In the third, write ten things that would still be true about you if every item in the first column disappeared tomorrow. Not what you do. Something about who is doing it.

If the third column is far harder to fill than the first, do not rush past that. It is showing you, precisely, where achievement has been asked to carry more than it was ever built to hold.

CHAPTER SIXTEEN

The Relational Self

✦

SHE HAD BEEN married for twenty three years when someone asked her what she wanted.

It was not a profound question. There was no therapist sitting across from her, no crisis unfolding, no major decision waiting to be made. She was having lunch with an old friend who was planning a trip and casually asked where she would go if she could choose anywhere for herself.

She opened her mouth and then stopped.

Her first thought was where her husband liked to travel. Her second was whether the children would want to come. Her third was how much everyone would be comfortable spending.

None of those thoughts were unreasonable. They were the ordinary calculations of a woman who had spent many years sharing a life with other people.

But her friend had not asked where the family should go. She had asked where she wanted to go. And she could not answer.

The question stayed with her long after lunch. Over the following days, she began noticing how often the same thing happened. What kind of food did she prefer? It depended on what everyone else wanted. What did she like doing on a completely free Saturday? She was not sure, Saturdays had not belonged only to her in years. What did she think about a decision her husband was considering? She knew what they thought, because they had already discussed it. She was less certain what she thought before the discussion began.

Nothing terrible had happened to her. She loved her husband. She loved her children. Her family was not controlling her. Nobody had ordered her to disappear.

That was what made the realization so difficult to explain. She had not lost herself in one dramatic moment. She had simply spent so many years becoming part of an us that she had stopped noticing how little attention she gave to the me inside it.

THE IDENTITY WE BUILD BETWEEN PEOPLE

Human beings are relational by nature. Much of who we become develops in connection with other people. We are daughters and sons, sisters and brothers, friends, spouses, parents, colleagues, neighbors, mentors, and members of communities. These relationships are not distractions from identity. They become part of its story.

There is something beautiful about this. Love changes us. Marriage changes us. Parenthood changes us. Friendship changes us. Living closely with another person teaches compromise, patience, sacrifice, generosity, and the difficult art of realizing that our preferences are not the only ones that matter.

A healthy identity is not an isolated identity.

The problem begins when relationship stops contributing to who we are and begins replacing who we are. The relational self is the version of identity that knows itself primarily through connection to another person. It does not simply say, this relationship matters deeply to me. It begins saying, often without words, I am not entirely sure who I am outside this relationship.

That can happen in romantic relationships, but it is not limited to them. A mother can build so much of herself around her children that their independence creates an identity crisis. Two close friends can become so emotionally intertwined that separate growth feels like betrayal. A person can become known almost entirely as someone's spouse, someone's daughter, someone's assistant, someone's partner, or someone's closest friend.

The relationship may be completely real. The love may be completely real. What has become unclear is where one life ends and the other begins.

When "We" Becomes the Only Pronoun

There is a natural progression in close relationships. Two separate lives begin sharing things. Our home. Our plans. Our friends. Our money. Our future. Our children. Our traditions. Our memories.

There is tenderness in the word our. It represents something that did not exist before two people chose to build it.

But healthy we does not require the death of I. You should still be able to know what you think before checking what the other person thinks. You should still have interests that belong to you, friendships you value, convictions you can explain, and parts of your inner life that have not simply been absorbed into the relationship.

This does not mean keeping secrets or living parallel lives. It means remaining a person while participating fully in partnership.

Some relationships become so close that difference begins to feel threatening. If one person changes an opinion, develops a new interest, forms a new friendship, or wants more independence, the other person experiences the change not as development but as distance. Why don't you want what we always wanted. You never used to think like this. Since when are you interested in that.

Sometimes these are innocent questions. Sometimes underneath them is another question entirely. If you become more yourself, what happens to us?

Love Does Not Require Sameness

One of the quiet myths inside some relationships is that closeness should produce sameness. We should enjoy the same things. Think the same way. Want the same amount of togetherness. Have the same friends. Reach conclusions at the same speed.

But two people can love each other deeply and remain different. One may need more quiet. The other enjoys constant company. One processes decisions by talking. The other needs time before speaking. One loves travel. The other prefers home.

Difference is not automatically distance. One of the marks of a mature relationship is its ability to contain two whole people without requiring either one to become a copy of the other. Immature closeness says, if you love me, you will become more like me. Mature closeness learns to say, I can remain connected to you without requiring you to stop being different from me. That is a harder kind of love. It is also a freer one.

BORROWED PREFERENCES

Sometimes losing yourself in relationship happens so gradually that it first appears in very small things.

You stop listening to music you enjoy because your partner dislikes it. You rarely see certain friends because they are not your spouse's favorite people. You stop pursuing an interest because nobody else in the family shares it. You always eat where the other person prefers. You arrange weekends around everybody else's enjoyment and can no longer remember what restores you.

None of these choices, by itself, necessarily means anything is wrong. Love involves compromise. Adults constantly adjust preferences for people they care about.

The question is not whether you compromise. The question is whether you still know what you compromised. There is a difference between saying, I would rather do something else, but this matters to you, so I am happy to come, and genuinely no longer knowing what you would rather do. The first is sacrifice. The second may be disappearance. You cannot consciously give something you have stopped knowing you possess.

Borrowed Opinions

Preferences are one thing. Opinions go deeper.

Some people become so accustomed to relational agreement that they begin checking another person's reaction before deciding what they themselves believe. A spouse tells a story and they adopt the spouse's interpretation. A close friend dislikes someone and gradually they dislike the person too. A parent strongly believes something and the adult child repeats the belief for years without ever examining whether it became their own.

Again, influence is normal. Every person you love will affect the way you see the world. But influence and surrender are different. There comes a point in adult identity when inherited and borrowed conclusions need to be examined. Do I actually believe this? Is this my conviction, or simply the safest opinion inside this relationship? Would I reach the same conclusion if this person were not in the room? Those questions are not acts of disloyalty. They are part of becoming an adult.

When Another Person's Mood Becomes Your Weather

The relational self does not only borrow preferences and opinions. Sometimes it borrows emotional states.

Your partner comes home irritated, and immediately you become anxious. Your mother sounds disappointed on the phone, and your entire evening changes. A friend becomes distant, and you cannot concentrate until you know why.

Close relationships naturally affect our emotions. If someone you love is hurting, you will often hurt with them. Emotional responsiveness is part of care. The difficulty begins when another person's emotional state becomes the controlling atmosphere of your own. If they are happy, you can relax. If they are upset, you cannot. If they approve, the day feels safe. If they withdraw, everything inside you becomes unsettled.

Eventually, you may become highly skilled at reading other people. A pause. A sigh. A facial expression. A slightly different tone. You notice the change before anyone else does. That sensitivity may look like extraordinary emotional intelligence, and sometimes it is. But sometimes it developed because your own sense of safety became too dependent on knowing what another person was feeling. You are not merely noticing the weather. You have begun living inside it.

The Relationship Becomes the Mirror

All of us learn something about ourselves through relationships. We discover that we are funny because people laugh with us. We discover strengths because others notice them. We learn where we need growth because people who love us sometimes tell us difficult truths.

Relationships are mirrors. The problem begins when one particular mirror becomes the only one you trust. If this person thinks I am beautiful, I feel beautiful. If this person desires me, I feel desirable. If this person is proud of me, I feel successful. If this person is disappointed in me, I begin doubting myself. If this person leaves me, I no longer know what that says about who I am.

At that point, the relationship has been given enormous authority. Love was meant to help us see ourselves more clearly. It was never meant to become the only place from which we are permitted to see ourselves at all.

The Couple Everyone Knows as a Couple

Some couples become almost inseparable in the minds of everyone around them. Their names are spoken together. Their invitations come together. Their routines are shared. Their social world overlaps almost completely.

There can be something beautiful about that kind of companionship. But even strong marriages contain two individual histories, two inner worlds, two sets of gifts, and two people who will continue developing across time. One of the healthiest questions inside a long relationship is not only, who are we becoming together. It is also, who are you becoming, and who am I becoming. Those questions protect the relationship from becoming a container too small for the people inside it.

A marriage does not become stronger because both people stop growing independently. Often it becomes stronger because each person is allowed to bring new life back into the shared one.

PARENTHOOD AND THE RELATIONAL SELF

Few relationships ask more from a person's identity than parenthood. For years, especially when children are young, life genuinely revolves around their needs. Their meals, health, education, transportation, activities, emotions, safety, and development consume enormous amounts of time and attention. This is not identity loss by definition. It is parenting.

But children grow. And when they do, some parents discover that the role expanded so completely that there is very little life waiting outside it. A mother may spend twenty five years organizing nearly every day around her children and then experience their independence as a strange emptiness. A father who built his sense of purpose around providing may struggle when adult children no longer need him in the same way.

The problem is not that they loved too much. Love is not the enemy here. The difficulty is that one role was asked to contain nearly the entire person. Healthy parenting eventually includes releasing, and release is easier when the parent has remained connected to a self that existed alongside the role. Your children need your love. They do not need to carry responsibility for giving you an identity once they grow up.

When a Relationship Ends and Takes the Self With It

The relational self often becomes most visible after loss. A relationship ends, through separation, divorce, death, estrangement, or simply two people whose lives gradually move in different directions.

The grief can be enormous because you are not only losing a person. You may be losing routines, friendships, traditions, plans, social roles, financial arrangements, places, habits, and an imagined future. Then another loss appears underneath all of them. The version of you that existed inside the relationship.

Someone who has been married for thirty years may suddenly have to make decisions alone that have always been made together. A person leaving a long relationship may realize that nearly every social connection belonged to the couple. Someone whose spouse dies may find themselves confronting simple questions they have not answered independently in decades. What do I do on Saturday. Where do I go for Christmas. Who are my people now. What do I enjoy. What do I want. Who am I if I am no longer us.

These questions do not mean the relationship was unhealthy. They reveal how deeply relationship becomes woven into identity. Grief sometimes includes the painful work of meeting yourself again.

Starting Over Without Starting From Nothing

After a major relationship ends, people sometimes say they have to start over. In one sense, they do. But you are not starting from nothing.

You bring everything you learned. The love you gave. The mistakes you made. The strength you discovered. The boundaries you now understand. The parts of yourself you neglected. The parts that grew. The things you will choose differently next time.

The relationship may have ended, but your life did not return to zero. Part of healing is separating what belonged to the relationship from what became part of you. Some things can be released. Some should be kept.

WHEN SEPARATION FEELS LIKE BETRAYAL

Relational identity can also make healthy independence feel disloyal. You begin pursuing something the other person does not understand. You need more time alone. You form friendships outside the shared circle. You return to school. Develop a career. Travel without the family. Begin exercising. Change your appearance. Explore an interest.

None of these things is automatically healthy or unhealthy. Context matters. But if every movement toward individual growth is interpreted as movement away from the relationship, both people can become trapped. A strong relationship should be able to survive reasonable expansion. Love should not require a person to remain exactly as they were when the relationship began.

The person you married at twenty eight will not be exactly the same at forty eight. Neither will you. The question is not whether people change. They will. The question is whether the relationship has enough room for both people to continue becoming.

THE DIFFERENCE BETWEEN INTIMACY AND FUSION

There is a kind of closeness that looks like intimacy but is actually the loss of emotional separation.

In genuine intimacy, two people can be deeply connected while still knowing what belongs to each of them. Your feelings matter to me, but I do not have to feel exactly what you feel. Your disappointment affects me, but it does not automatically mean I have done something wrong. Your opinion matters, but it does not replace mine. Your dream deserves respect, but I am not required to make it my dream. Your struggle may call for my support, but I cannot live your life for you.

This is what allows closeness without disappearance. Without that separation, love can slowly turn into management. Each person becomes responsible for regulating the other. One cannot be disappointed because the other cannot tolerate the disappointment. One cannot disagree because disagreement feels like abandonment. One cannot change because change threatens the shared identity. The relationship becomes close, but not necessarily free.

Healthy intimacy says, I can be close enough to know you deeply without becoming responsible for being you.

THE DANGER OF MAKING ONE PERSON YOUR ENTIRE WORLD

Romantic language sometimes celebrates the idea that one person should be everything. Best friend. Confidant. Companion. Emotional support. Social life. Source of affirmation. Source of adventure. Source of belonging. Source of meaning.

It sounds romantic. It is also an enormous job description. No single human being can sustainably meet every relational need another person has.

Healthy relationships usually exist within a larger life. Friends. Family. Community. Meaningful work. Interests. Purpose. Time alone. Different people bring different kinds of connection. When one person becomes the entire emotional world, ordinary changes in that relationship become catastrophic because there is nowhere else inside the life for the self to stand.

This does not make the relationship less important. It makes the person larger than the relationship.

A RELATIONSHIP SHOULD ADD TO A LIFE, NOT SWALLOW IT

There are relationships in which people become more themselves. They become braver, more curious, more peaceful, more honest. They discover interests, develop gifts, heal, learn. The relationship creates enough safety for both people to expand.

There are other relationships in which one or both people slowly contract. They stop doing things they once loved. Lose friendships. Silence opinions. Reduce dreams. Avoid growth that might disturb the relationship.

The difference is worth noticing. Love will sometimes require sacrifice. Every lasting relationship does. But healthy sacrifice is different from chronic disappearance. Sacrifice says, something matters enough that I am choosing to give something for it. Disappearance says, there is increasingly less of me left to choose.

Two Becoming One Does Not Mean Two Becoming One Person

There is an old and familiar description of marriage worth returning to here, two becoming one. It has sometimes been misunderstood as though healthy love requires two identities to dissolve into a single personality.

But unity is not erasure. Two becoming one was never meant to describe two people becoming one person. The strength of union is precisely that two distinct lives choose faithfulness, shared purpose, mutual care, and deep connection, while remaining two distinct lives underneath the choosing. The same wisdom that honors unity also has a great deal to say about individual responsibility, personal gifts, and the unique life each person has been given to steward. There is no contradiction there. Healthy relationship holds both truths at once. I belong with you. And I remain responsible for the person I bring into that belonging.

Returning to Yourself Without Leaving the Relationship

The woman from the beginning of this chapter did not go home from lunch and announce that she needed to rediscover herself. She did not leave her family. She did not blame her husband. There was nothing dramatic to fix.

Instead, she began paying attention. She noticed that she still loved old jazz records she had barely listened to in years. She remembered that before the children were born she used to visit galleries alone, slowly, because she liked being able to stand in front of one painting for as long as she wanted. She called a friend she had not seen without their husbands present in nearly two years.

When her husband asked where she wanted to eat one evening, she almost said, anywhere is fine, and then stopped herself. There is actually somewhere I want to try.

He looked surprised. Then he smiled. Okay.

Nothing broke. That became part of the lesson. She had assumed, without ever examining the assumption, that being a loving wife and mother meant becoming endlessly flexible around everybody else's preferences. Nobody had actually asked that of her.

Some of her disappearance had happened through love. Some through habit. Some through the ordinary demands of family life. And some through her own failure to keep asking a simple question. What is true for me too.

She began asking it again. Not instead of us. Inside it. That distinction mattered. She did not need to become less connected in order to become more herself. She simply needed to remember that the relationship contained her too.

THE GOAL IS NOT INDEPENDENCE FROM LOVE

Identity healing can easily swing too far. A person realizes they have lost themselves in relationships and decides the answer is needing nobody. That is not wholeness. It is often hurt protecting itself.

The goal is not to become unreachable, emotionally self sufficient, or suspicious of dependence. Human beings need one another. There will be seasons when you lean heavily on someone else and seasons when they lean heavily on you. There will be relationships that shape your life so deeply that losing them changes you permanently. That is not weakness.

The goal is not independence from relationship. It is enough inner rootedness that love can connect you without consuming you. You can say we without losing I. You can belong deeply without disappearing. You can allow another person's life to matter enormously without making it the only place your own life receives meaning. And you can love someone enough to grow beside them instead of slowly becoming invisible inside them.

✦

SOUL MIRROR

If one of your major relational roles changed tomorrow, spouse, parent, caregiver, closest friend, who would you still know yourself to be?

TIMELESS WISDOM

The deepest relationships do not require two people to become one personality. Love creates connection without demanding disappearance. A healthy relationship gives you somewhere to belong while still leaving you enough room to become.

RENEWAL PRACTICE: Finding the "I" Inside the "We"

Take a page and divide it into three sections.

In the first, write what belongs to us: the responsibilities, goals, traditions, finances, and commitments you genuinely share with the important people in your life.

In the second, write what still belongs to me: your personal interests, convictions, friendships, dreams, and the ways you restore yourself that do not need to be identical to anyone else's.

In the third, write what you have quietly given up. Some things may have been wisely sacrificed. Life requires that. But others may have disappeared without any real decision being made. Choose one thing from that final list that still matters to you, and ask, without any dramatic announcement, how it might have a healthy place in your life again.

Then finish with this sentence. I do not have to choose between loving people deeply and remaining a person of my own. Healthy love has room for both.

CHAPTER SEVENTEEN

The Wounded Self

✦

FOR MOST OF her adult life, she described herself as someone who did not trust easily.

She said it casually, almost as though she were describing the color of her eyes. People had disappointed her too many times, and experience had taught her to be careful. She did not expect much from anyone, did not become emotionally dependent, and rarely shared anything she could not handle becoming public. When people described her as guarded, she usually agreed. She considered it one of the wiser things life had taught her.

The explanation made sense because there was history behind it.

Her father had left when she was eleven. Not completely, but inconsistently enough that every promise became uncertain. He would say he was coming and sometimes never arrive. He remembered birthdays some years and forgot them in others. She learned not to become too excited when he made plans because excitement made disappointment hurt more.

At twenty four, she became engaged to a man she trusted completely. Six months before the wedding, she discovered that he had been involved with someone else for most of their engagement. The relationship ended, but the experience seemed to confirm something she had already learned much earlier: people could say they loved you and still leave you standing somewhere waiting for them.

By thirty eight, she had built a good life. She was professionally successful, financially responsible, socially connected, and generally well liked. She was not living in obvious emotional distress. Yet almost every close relationship had to pass through a security system built from experiences that had happened years before.

People who had never abandoned her were required to prove they would not. People who had never betrayed her were treated with the caution created by someone who had.

She thought she was simply being wise.

What she had not considered was that pain had become one of the authors of her personality.

WHAT HAPPENS TO US DOES NOT STAY IN THE PAST

When people speak about painful experiences, they often talk about them as though the event and its effects occupy the same period of time. Something happened five years ago, so we naturally think of it as belonging to five years ago.

Emotionally, life is not always that tidy. An event can end while the meaning we gave it continues. The relationship ended, but the belief that people cannot be trusted remained. The bullying stopped, but the expectation of humiliation followed the child into adulthood. The financial crisis passed, but the fear of losing everything continued long after stability returned. The parent stopped criticizing, perhaps even died, but the adult child continued hearing the criticism internally whenever they made a mistake.

This is one reason simply saying, that happened a long time ago, rarely settles emotional pain. Time creates distance from an event, but distance alone does not determine what the event came to mean.

The wound is not only what happened. It is also what you concluded because it happened.

A child whose parent leaves may conclude that people leave. Another may conclude that they were not worth staying for. A person who is repeatedly mocked may conclude that visibility is dangerous.

Someone betrayed by a partner may conclude that trust is foolish. A person raised in constant criticism may conclude that mistakes make love uncertain.

Those conclusions may never be spoken aloud, but they can become deeply influential because they begin shaping how future experiences are interpreted.

WHEN PAIN STARTS ANSWERING "WHO AM I?"

There is an important difference between carrying a wound and becoming identified with it.

A wound says, something painful happened to me. The wounded self begins saying, what happened tells me something permanent about who I am.

Rejection becomes I am unwanted. Betrayal becomes I am foolish for trusting. Abandonment becomes I am someone people eventually leave. Abuse becomes I am powerless. Repeated criticism becomes I am never quite good enough. Being ignored becomes my needs do not matter.

These conclusions often feel true because they were formed through real experience. This is what makes them difficult to challenge. We are not dealing with imaginary events. Something actually happened. The person really did leave. The betrayal really occurred. The words really were spoken. The humiliation was real.

Healing does not require pretending otherwise. It does not ask us to rewrite history into something pleasant so that we can feel better about it.

The deeper work is learning to separate two questions that pain often joins together: what happened to me, and what does what happened mean about me. Those questions are not the same.

THE MEANING WE ATTACH TO PAIN

Two people can experience similar events and carry very different conclusions from them.

Imagine two children whose parents divorce. One child may quietly decide, relationships do not last. Another may decide, dad left because I was difficult. A third may conclude, I need to take care of Mom now. A fourth may become determined never to depend on anyone.

The event is similar. The identity conclusions are different.

This matters because people often spend years trying to manage the consequences of a wound without examining the meaning attached to it. The person who believes people always leave may become extremely independent. The person who believes they caused the loss may become a pleaser. The child who became responsible for a struggling parent may grow into the adult who carries everyone. Someone who concluded that vulnerability is dangerous may become the strong person who never asks for help.

The behavior makes more sense once we understand the belief beneath it. Instead of asking only, why do I keep doing this, it can be more helpful to ask, what did I learn that made this behavior feel necessary. That question moves us away from judgment and toward understanding.

PROTECTION IS OFTEN BUILT AROUND THE WOUND

Human beings adapt. When something hurts us, we naturally try to reduce the possibility of experiencing the same pain again. This is not weakness. It is part of survival.

A child who is frequently criticized may become unusually careful. Someone who has been betrayed may become observant and slow to trust. A person who grew up around unpredictable anger may become highly sensitive to changes in people's moods. Someone who experienced financial instability may become disciplined about money.

These adaptations can become genuine strengths. Carefulness can produce excellence. Sensitivity can create compassion. Financial caution can produce stability. Independence can create remarkable competence.

This is why healing is more complicated than simply removing unhealthy behavior. Sometimes the behavior that now limits us also helped us survive an earlier season. We may even be proud of it.

The question is not whether the adaptation was foolish. It may have been remarkably intelligent for the circumstances in which it developed. The question is whether those circumstances still exist.

A protection that was necessary at twelve may become restrictive at forty. The emotional wall that kept one dangerous person out may later keep trustworthy people out as well. The refusal to need anyone may protect against abandonment while also preventing intimacy. Constant vigilance may reduce the chance of being surprised, but it may also make peace almost impossible.

Protection can remain long after the original danger has passed.

When the Past Starts Predicting the Future

One of the most powerful effects of unresolved pain is that it begins making predictions. You meet someone new, but the past is already in the room.

A partner becomes quiet, and you remember someone who used silence as punishment. A supervisor asks to speak with you, and your body reacts as though you are about to be humiliated. A friend cancels plans twice, and something inside you moves quickly from disappointment to the certainty that the friendship is ending. A particular tone of voice, an anniversary, a smell, or even a facial expression can awaken emotions that seem much larger than the immediate situation.

The current event may deserve attention. Sometimes the concern is accurate. People do repeat harmful patterns, and wisdom should not require ignoring warning signs. But sometimes the present is being interpreted entirely through an old wound, and the wounded self does not simply remember what happened. It expects what happened to happen again.

People sometimes become embarrassed by how large the reaction feels, and tell themselves they are overreacting or should have moved on by now. A more useful response is curiosity rather than embarrassment. Why did this particular moment affect me so strongly. What did it remind me of. What did I immediately assume was about to happen.

The feeling is real, but the prediction attached to the feeling may not be. Feeling abandoned does not necessarily mean you are currently being abandoned. Feeling unsafe does not automatically mean the present person is unsafe. Feeling rejected does not prove that rejection is occurring. Our emotions provide important information, but they do not always provide the complete interpretation. Healing involves learning to listen to the feeling without automatically allowing the feeling to write the conclusion.

THE PERSON WHO HURT YOU IS NOT EVERYONE

One of the most costly things pain can do is turn one person's behavior into a rule about human beings.

A dishonest partner becomes evidence that nobody can be trusted. A controlling parent becomes evidence that closeness always costs freedom. A cruel friend becomes evidence that vulnerability will eventually be used against you. A manipulative leader becomes evidence that authority itself is dangerous.

The conclusion is understandable because general rules create a sense of protection. If you assume everyone is dangerous, you may believe you are less likely to be surprised by danger.

But generalizing pain creates another problem. It gives people who never hurt you consequences they did not create. A future partner may spend years paying for a betrayal committed by someone they have never met. A trustworthy friend may be kept at emotional distance because an earlier friend mishandled vulnerability. A healthy leader may be treated with suspicion because a previous authority figure abused power.

Wisdom remembers. But wisdom also distinguishes. Healing does not require trusting everyone. It requires learning that everyone is not the person who wounded you.

WHEN PAIN BECOMES PERSONALITY

After enough years, protective patterns can become so familiar that we stop recognizing them as adaptations. We simply say, this is who I am. I am private. I do not trust easily. I hate depending on people. I never cry. I always expect the worst. I do not need anybody.

Some of these statements may describe genuine personality. Not every private person is wounded. Not every independent person is avoiding vulnerability. Personality differences are real.

But it is worth asking whether certain traits are entirely personality or partly protection. Would I still be this guarded if nobody had betrayed me. Would I still find receiving help this uncomfortable if dependence had not once been used against me. Would I still assume criticism is rejection if mistakes had been handled differently when I was young. Would I still avoid conflict if conflict had not once become frightening.

The purpose of these questions is not to dismantle your personality. It is to discover whether pain has been allowed to name parts of you that may actually be defenses rather than identity.

THE WOUND CAN BECOME THE CENTER OF THE STORY

Pain deserves to be acknowledged. Some experiences are life changing, and language that minimizes them can become another injury.

But there is also a danger in allowing the wound to become the central explanation for everything. Eventually every difficulty is traced back to what happened. Every relationship is interpreted through it. Every limitation is explained by it. The wound becomes not merely an important chapter of the story but the title of the entire book.

This can happen especially when a person finally finds language for something they endured. Understanding can initially bring enormous relief. Experiences that once felt confusing begin making sense. Patterns become visible. The person realizes that certain reactions have a history. That recognition is valuable. But insight is supposed to open a door, not become another room we live in permanently.

There is a difference between saying, now I understand why I became this way, and saying, because this happened, this is simply who I will always be. The first creates possibility. The second turns explanation into destiny.

FEAR OF DISHONORING WHAT YOU SURVIVED

People sometimes fear that moving beyond a wound means minimizing it. If I stop identifying myself through what happened, am I saying it did not matter. If I forgive, does that mean it was acceptable. If I become happy again, am I betraying the seriousness of what I survived.

These are understandable concerns, but healing does not require dishonoring pain. You can say, this changed me, without saying, this owns me. You can acknowledge that an experience affected your relationships, confidence, expectations, and choices while still believing that your future can become larger than its consequences. You can remember without living permanently inside the memory.

WHEN THE WOUND BRINGS GIFTS YOU NEVER ASKED FOR

Pain does not automatically make people better. Suffering can make someone compassionate, but it can also make them bitter. It can produce wisdom, but it can also produce fear. We should be careful about romanticizing painful experiences as though people needed to be hurt in order to become valuable.

You did not need betrayal in order to deserve wisdom. You did not need abuse in order to become strong. You did not need abandonment in order to become compassionate.

Yet human beings have a remarkable ability to develop something meaningful even from experiences they would never have chosen. A person who knows rejection may become unusually attentive to people standing alone in a room. Someone who grew up unheard may become an excellent listener. A person who experienced financial instability may become thoughtful about creating security for others.

These qualities do not make the wound good. They show that the wound did not get the final word. There is an important difference.

Healing Is Not Becoming the Person You Were Before

People often speak about healing as getting back to myself. Sometimes that language is helpful. But there are wounds after which there is no previous self to return to. The experience may have happened in childhood, before identity was fully formed. Or the loss may have changed life permanently. A person whose spouse dies after thirty years of marriage cannot simply return to the person they were before the marriage.

Healing is not always restoration to an earlier version of you. Sometimes it is integration. You learn how to carry what happened without allowing it to control everything that happens next. You keep the wisdom without keeping every defense. You honor what you survived without requiring survival to remain your primary identity.

The healed self is not necessarily the unwounded self. It is the self that can acknowledge the wound without being organized around it.

The Body Sometimes Remembers What the Mind Has Explained

We can understand something intellectually and still react to it emotionally.

You may know that the current relationship is safe and still feel anxious during conflict. You may understand that your supervisor is not your critical parent and still feel unusually distressed by correction. This does not mean the healing work has failed. Human beings are not only thinking creatures. Experiences are carried through habits, emotions, expectations, and physical responses as well as conscious memory.

This is one reason healing often requires patience. Sometimes the mind learns a new truth before the rest of us becomes comfortable living inside it. A person who has spent twenty years expecting abandonment may not become secure simply because they finally understand where the fear came from. Understanding matters, but new experiences matter too. Trustworthy people have to remain trustworthy long enough for the nervous system to encounter something different. Healing often grows through repeated evidence that the present does not have to reproduce the past.

THE COURAGE TO STOP PROTECTING AN OLD VERSION OF YOU

There may come a point when the protection itself becomes more costly than the possibility of being hurt again. This does not mean becoming careless. A healed person still has boundaries, still notices warning signs, still leaves unsafe situations, still understands that forgiveness and access are not the same thing.

But healthy protection becomes flexible. It responds to what is actually happening rather than assuming the old danger is everywhere. You begin allowing trustworthy people closer. You say what you need instead of expecting people to guess. You let yourself hope without demanding a guarantee that disappointment will never happen. You participate in life again.

That is one of the hardest parts of healing because the wounded self often believes safety can be achieved only by reducing vulnerability. But complete protection from pain would require complete protection from life. You cannot guarantee that nobody will disappoint you again. You can become strong enough to know that disappointment does not have to destroy your identity.

NEAR, NOT ABSENT

There is an old and comforting picture worth holding onto here, one that does not treat woundedness as shameful or imaginary. It speaks openly about broken hearts, grief, betrayal, and the need for restoration, and it does not ask anyone to deny pain in order to hold onto hope. One of its steadiest claims is that nearness arrives precisely in brokenness, not after it has been tidied away.

Brokenness is acknowledged there, but it is never presented as abandonment. The wound is seen, but the person is never reduced to it. What was broken can be tended. What was lost can be grieved. What became distorted can be renewed, and a life can continue with real meaning beyond the place where the pain first entered it. That is different from denying the wound. It is refusing to let the wound have the final word.

MEETING THE WOMAN WHO DID NOT TRUST

The woman who had spent most of her adult life saying that she did not trust easily did not suddenly become trusting. That would not have been healing. It would have been another extreme.

What changed first was her language. She stopped saying, I am just someone who doesn't trust people, as though distrust were an unchangeable feature of her identity. Instead, she began saying something more accurate: I learned to be very careful about trust because some important people were unreliable.

The difference sounded small, but it changed the story. The first statement described who she was. The second described what she had learned. And what has been learned can be examined.

She began noticing how quickly she withdrew when someone disappointed her. She noticed that she sometimes tested people without telling them there was a test, withholding something small, waiting to see whether they noticed, and interpreting their failure to notice as evidence that they did not really care. She had been gathering proof for a conclusion she already believed.

Slowly, she tried something different. She told a close friend when something had hurt her instead of becoming distant. The friend apologized. She allowed someone to help her with something she could technically have handled alone. Nothing was demanded in return. She entered another relationship eventually, and when fear appeared, she tried to distinguish between what the man in front of her was actually doing and what someone else had done years earlier. Sometimes the distinction was easy. Sometimes it was not.

Healing did not erase her history. She still valued consistency. She still believed trust should be earned. She was still more observant than some people. But gradually those qualities stopped functioning as guards standing permanently at the door. They became wisdom she could use rather than walls she had to live behind.

For years she had believed the wound made her who she was. Eventually she understood something gentler and more accurate. The wound had shaped her. It had not been given ownership of her.

A scar is evidence that something happened. It is not evidence that the wound is still open.

✦

SOUL MIRROR

Think of one experience that changed how you relate to yourself or other people, something you can examine honestly without overwhelming yourself. What did you begin believing because it happened, and which behaviors in your life today may have started as protection against feeling that way again?

TIMELESS WISDOM

Pain can shape identity without having the right to define it. What happened to you belongs to your story. It does not have to become your name.

RENEWAL PRACTICE: Separating the Wound From the Self

Write briefly about one experience that continues to influence how you see yourself, other people, or life. You do not need to relive every detail, only enough to identify what happened and why it mattered.

Then complete four statements in full sentences.

Because this happened, I began believing that. Write the conclusion you carried away from the experience.

Because I believed this, I learned to protect myself by. Identify what you began doing. Perhaps you became independent, guarded, pleasing, controlling, quiet, suspicious, or determined never to need help.

This protection helped me by. Do not skip this part. Before criticizing an old defense, acknowledge why it existed. It may have helped you survive something difficult.

Today, this same protection costs me. Consider relationships, peace, opportunities, emotional freedom, intimacy, or anything else it may now be affecting.

Read what you have written and ask one final question. What would a wiser form of protection look like in my life now. Perhaps it is not trusting everybody, but learning to recognize trustworthy people. Perhaps it is not refusing to depend on anyone, but becoming more careful about whom you depend upon.

The goal is not to make yourself vulnerable to the same harm again. The goal is to stop requiring your present life to live permanently under rules written during one of the most painful periods of your past. You are allowed to keep the wisdom. You do not have to keep the wound in charge.

C H A P T E R   E I G H T E E N

The Strong One

✦

SHE WAS FIFTY-EIGHT, and she drove herself home from the hospital.

Four people had offered. Her sister. Her neighbor. Two women from church. She thanked every one of them warmly and said she was fine, it was covered, someone was taking her, which was true, in a way. Someone was. She was.

The operation had gone well. The nurse said take it easy for a fortnight. She stopped at the shop on the way home because there was no bread in the house.

That evening she sat in the kitchen with the light off. She had been meaning to make something to eat for about an hour and a half and had not managed to stand up. At some point she realised she was crying. Not the kind that passes. The kind that comes from somewhere lower down. She had not cried in three years.

What surprised her was not the crying.

It was the sentence that came with it.

Not *I need help.*

What is wrong with me that I can't manage this?

✦

Some people were never given permission to be weak.

It usually starts young. Something happens, an illness, a separation, money running out, a parent who couldn't cope. And a child works out, without anyone explaining it, that somebody in this house has to hold things together.

So they do.

Nobody sits a child down and hands them the job. It arrives quietly. A mother who cries at the kitchen table and a nine-year-old who learns to make tea and say nothing about it at school. An older sister who gets the younger ones dressed because their mother is on nights. A boy who stops mentioning the thing that frightens him, because his father already looks tired.

And here is the part that matters. It works.

The child is praised for it. *She's so mature for her age. He's no trouble at all. I don't know what I'd do without you.* The praise is genuine. The relief behind it is genuine too. And the child, who is paying attention the way children always are, draws the obvious conclusion.

This is what makes me valuable. This is what I'm for.

That is not a bad conclusion. Given the house they were standing in, it may have been the only sensible one available. Every identity in this part of the book began as a solution to a real problem. That is why they are so hard to see. They are not mistakes. They are things that worked.

But a child grows up, and the house changes, and the strategy doesn't.

✦

Twenty years on, the strong one is the person everybody calls.

They're the one who remembers birthdays and knows where the paperwork is. The one who gets phoned when there's bad news, because they'll know what to do. The one who books the taxi, chases the doctor, sits with the relative nobody else can manage, and then goes to work in the morning.

They are usually good at this. That is not a small thing. There is real capability here and it should be said plainly, because so much of what follows will sound like criticism and it is not. These are frequently the most useful people in any family, any workplace, any church. Take them out and things fall over.

But somewhere along the way, being strong stopped being something they do.

It became who they are.

And you can tell the difference, because when strength becomes an identity it starts having rules. It can't be put down for an evening. It doesn't have days off. It cannot admit to struggling without something inside going off like an alarm. The strong person does not experience these as rules. They experience them as facts about themselves. *I'm just not someone who falls apart.*

✦

There is a strange consequence to being this person, and it is one of the loneliest things in this book.

Nobody checks on you.

Not out of coldness. Out of arithmetic. People have limited worry, and they spend it where it seems needed. So they spend it on the sibling who is in trouble, the friend going through a divorce, the colleague who is clearly not coping. And the one who is always fine gets a completely different kind of attention: admiration, reliance, gratitude. All of it warm. None of it care.

Everyone in the family is all right, and the reason everyone is all right is standing in the kitchen at eleven at night doing the last of the washing up.

Ask them how they are and they will tell you about somebody else.

✦

Now here is the test, and it is the only diagnostic this chapter needs.

Offer them help. Then watch what happens.

They will thank you and decline. Warmly, they are not cold people, and with a reason ready, because they have had the reason prepared since before you asked.

Press a little, and something shifts. Guilt arrives. *No, honestly, you've got enough on.* They will start managing your feelings about their refusal.

Insist, and you will see something you were not expecting. Not gratitude. Something closer to panic. Because if they let you carry this, then they are a person who needed carrying, and they have no idea who that person is or whether anyone would stay for her.

They are not being humble. It looks like humility. It gets praised as selflessness and sometimes as faith. But humility can receive. Humility can say *yes, thank you, I'm struggling, would you.* What is happening here is not humility. It is a door that only opens one way.

They will give you anything. They cannot let you give them a lift home.

✦

Ask them who holds them and watch how long the pause is.

Most will not have an answer. Some will name someone, and then, if the room is quiet and they are being honest, they will add that the person doesn't really know, not the whole of it, not the worst week, not the thing they have never said to anyone.

Ask a further question, gently: when did you decide that was all right?

Because there was a moment. There is always a moment, usually early, usually so ordinary that nobody else in the room noticed. A time they reached for someone and nobody was free. A time they said something true and it made things worse. A time they were the one crying and the house needed them not to be.

And they filed it. *Right. So that's not available to me.*

Then they built a whole life on top of the filing.

✦

Which brings us to what nobody warns them about.

When the strong one finally goes down, it comes without warning. Not because there were no signs, but because the signs were switched off years ago. This is a person who stopped reporting tiredness at about fourteen. Who does not really know what they are feeling, because feeling it was never one of the options. The instrument panel was disconnected a long time ago, and so the engine gives no warning at all. It simply stops.

It rarely looks dramatic. More often it is this: someone competent, admired, entirely on top of things, sitting in a dark kitchen unable to stand up and make food, wondering what is wrong with them.

That is not weakness arriving.

That is the bill.

✦

There is an old story about a prophet named Elijah that has always seemed to me to belong to these people.

He had just done the most extraordinary thing of his career. A public triumph, in front of everybody, the kind of day that makes a reputation permanent. And immediately afterwards he walked out into the desert, sat down under a tree, and asked God to let him die.

What happens next is the part worth sitting with.

He is not corrected. He is not asked to explain himself, or reminded of what he had achieved the previous week, or told to be strong. He is allowed to sleep. Then he is given something to eat. Then he is allowed to sleep again, and given something to eat again.

Only after that does anyone say a word to him about anything.

Whatever else you believe about that story, notice the order of it. Food and rest came first. The words came a long way afterwards, and they were gentle when they came. The greatest thing this man ever did was followed by the worst hour of his life, and heaven's first response was a meal and a nap.

There is a whole theology of being human in that, and it is this: you are not a machine, and you were never expected to be one.

✦

So what changes?

Not the strength. That is worth saying clearly, because the strong one always assumes this is the part where they are asked to stop being capable, and they will refuse, and rightly. Their strength is real. It has held real things up. Nobody is asking for it back.

What changes is whether it can be set down.

There is a difference between being able to carry something and being unable to put it down. One is capacity. The other is compulsion, and it only looks like capacity from the outside. A person with genuine strength can say: not this time. Not this one. I've got nothing left this week. And they can say it without an explanation, without earning it first, and without spending three days making up for it afterwards.

That is not the opposite of strength.

That is the version of it that lasts.

✦

You were not born the strong one.

You became it, because at some point somebody had to be, and you were the one paying attention. That was not a character flaw. In all likelihood it was the most useful thing anybody in that house did, and much of what your family has, they have because you carried it.

But the child who took that on was not given a choice, and you are not a child any more.

You are allowed to find out whether you are loved for something other than what you hold up.

✦

SOUL MIRROR

Who holds you?

And if the answer is no one, when did you decide that was acceptable?

TIMELESS WISDOM

Strength that cannot rest is not strength. It is fear that has learned to look impressive.

RENEWAL PRACTICE: Let Somebody

This week, accept one offer of help you would normally turn down.

It does not need to be a large one. A lift. A meal. Someone carrying something. The size is not the point.

Three rules, and they are the whole exercise:

Do not pay it back. Do not play it down. Do not apologise for it.

Afterwards, write three things.

What you felt while it was happening.

What you were certain the other person was feeling.

And, if you can find out, what they actually said.

The distance between the last two is the size of the thing you have been believing.

CHAPTER NINETEEN

The Invisible Self

✦

FOR ALMOST FIFTEEN years, nobody in the office had anything bad to say about him.

He was dependable, courteous, and easy to work with. He rarely complained. He did not involve himself in workplace drama, did not compete aggressively for attention, and could usually be counted on to complete whatever was assigned to him without creating unnecessary problems.

When disagreements arose in meetings, he listened. When someone interrupted him, he usually let them continue. When he had an idea but another person seemed more confident, he often decided that the idea was probably not important enough to insist upon. He had watched louder colleagues receive recognition for suggestions similar to ones he had made quietly weeks earlier, but he rarely challenged it.

He told himself that he did not care about recognition. For many years, he almost believed it.

Then the company appointed a new departmental director. During their first individual meeting, she asked about his career plans.

He gave the usual answers about supporting the department, continuing to develop professionally, and being willing to contribute wherever he was needed.

She listened for a while before interrupting him.

I understand what the department needs, she said. I'm asking what you want.

He was surprised by how difficult the question felt.

He had ambitions. He knew that. There were positions he had imagined himself holding and ideas he had wanted to develop. Yet sitting across from someone who had directly invited him to speak about himself, he struggled to find language that did not immediately turn the conversation back toward what other people needed.

His director noticed. You seem very comfortable contributing, she said. You seem much less comfortable being seen contributing.

The sentence followed him home.

It was not the first time someone had noticed this about him. His wife had complained for years that he allowed people to overlook him. Friends had encouraged him to speak up more. He had always interpreted their comments as differences in personality. He was simply quieter than some people. He did not need attention. He preferred staying in the background.

Some of that was true. But not all of it.

The more honestly he examined his life, the more he began to recognize a distinction he had never considered before. There was a difference between being a quiet person and believing that taking up space was somehow inappropriate.

LEARNING NOT TO BE A PROBLEM

Some people grow up receiving the message that their presence is welcome. They can ask questions, express needs, make mistakes, disagree, become excited, cry, laugh loudly, and occupy emotional space without feeling that their presence itself creates a problem.

Others learn something different, and sometimes nobody teaches the lesson deliberately. It develops through circumstances.

A child grows up in a household already overwhelmed by financial problems, illness, marital conflict, addiction, grief, or another struggling child. They notice that the adults have more than enough to manage, so they become unusually undemanding. They learn to entertain themselves. They stop asking for things. They become careful about bringing problems home. When asked whether everything is all right, they say yes because adding another difficulty to the household feels inconsiderate.

In another family, visibility attracts criticism. The child who speaks too confidently is corrected for showing off. The child who expresses a strong opinion is told not to be disrespectful. Achievement may be welcomed as long as it does not appear prideful.

Other children become invisible for social reasons. They are bullied when noticed, embarrassed in classrooms, mocked for their appearance, accent, intelligence, family circumstances, or personality. Eventually they discover that avoiding attention reduces opportunities for humiliation.

The lesson takes different forms, but it often arrives at the same conclusion: life is easier when I do not attract too much attention to myself. That conclusion may begin as protection. Eventually it can become identity.

INVISIBILITY IS NOT THE SAME AS INTROVERSION

It is important not to confuse invisibility with a quiet personality.

Some people genuinely prefer less social stimulation. They think before speaking, enjoy solitude, dislike being the center of attention, and would rather have a meaningful conversation with one person than circulate through a crowded room. Nothing about this needs fixing.

The invisible self is different. The difference is not primarily how much you speak. It is what happens inside you when being seen becomes necessary.

A quiet person can still state an opinion when it matters. They can ask for what they need, accept recognition, establish boundaries, correct a misunderstanding, and allow their work to be acknowledged. They may not enjoy attention, but attention does not threaten their sense of legitimacy.

The invisible person often experiences something more complicated. Speaking up can feel presumptuous. Asking for something can feel demanding. Receiving praise can produce an immediate urge to minimize the accomplishment. The issue is not volume. It is permission. Somewhere along the way, the person learned that other people naturally occupy space while they must justify doing so.

THE HABIT OF MAKING YOURSELF SMALLER

Self erasure usually appears in ordinary moments before it appears in major ones.

Someone asks where you would like to eat, and you automatically say that anywhere is fine. A colleague presents an idea that originated partly with you, and you decide it would be awkward to clarify your contribution. Someone repeatedly mispronounces your name, but you stop correcting them because you do not want to embarrass them.

You receive a compliment and immediately explain why the accomplishment was not particularly impressive. You are interrupted in conversation and abandon the sentence rather than returning to it. You need something from someone but spend so much time explaining why it is not a big deal that the request almost disappears inside the explanation.

Each incident seems small. Taken together, they can reveal a pattern in which the person repeatedly reduces themselves to make interactions easier for everyone else.

This is different from humility. Humility does not require pretending you have nothing valuable to contribute. It does not require denying competence, silencing reasonable needs, or allowing other people to receive credit for your work. Humility gives us an accurate view of ourselves. Self erasure gives us a diminished one. There is nothing humble about believing everyone else deserves room that you do not.

THE PERSON NOBODY WORRIES ABOUT

Invisible people are often described as easy. Easy child. Easy employee. Easy friend. Easy partner. They do not require much attention. They adapt quickly. They rarely create conflict.

Being easy to live with can certainly be a virtue. Nobody benefits from turning every preference into a demand. But there is a hidden cost when being easy becomes the only acceptable way to be loved. The person begins filtering needs according to how inconvenient they might be for someone else, tolerating discomfort far longer than necessary because raising the issue would disturb the atmosphere.

Eventually the people around them become accustomed to their low level of demand. Then something painful can happen. The invisible person begins wondering why nobody notices them. Why does nobody ask what I need. Why does everyone assume I will be fine.

Sometimes the answer is that the people around them have genuinely become inconsiderate. But sometimes the answer is more complicated. Everyone has been trained by years of interaction to believe the message the invisible person has repeatedly communicated: do not worry about me. The tragedy is that the message may never have been true.

WHEN YOU STOP EXPECTING TO BE ASKED

There is a particular kind of disappointment that develops when people repeatedly feel overlooked. At first they hope someone will notice, that a parent will ask what is wrong without being told, that a partner will recognize how exhausted they are.

When this does not happen consistently, expectation begins to shrink. Eventually the person may stop asking because they have already decided what the answer will be. This is where invisibility becomes self reinforcing. The person expects not to be noticed, so they reveal less. Because they reveal less, other people have less information with which to notice them. When others fail to respond to needs that were never expressed, the original belief feels confirmed. Nobody sees me.

The conclusion may contain real history. But the pattern becomes dangerous when people in the present are required to pass tests they do not know they are taking. Being seen sometimes requires becoming visible, and adult relationships cannot depend entirely on others correctly interpreting what we refuse to communicate. There comes a point when healing requires giving trustworthy people information they could not otherwise know.

THE FEAR OF BEING TOO MUCH

Many invisible people carry a quiet fear that if they became fully visible, they would become excessive. Too emotional. Too opinionated. Too needy. Too ambitious. Too loud.

Perhaps someone actually used these words. Perhaps the message was communicated indirectly through sighs, withdrawal, or repeated praise for being the child who never caused trouble.

The result can be an adult who carefully manages how much of themselves enters every room. They may reveal sadness, but only after making it clear that they will be fine. They express an opinion, but soften it repeatedly so nobody mistakes conviction for arrogance. They share an accomplishment and immediately redirect attention elsewhere. This constant editing creates a strange form of exhaustion because the person is not simply participating in life. They are continuously calculating how much of themselves other people can tolerate. The deeper question is rarely whether they are actually too much. It is why they became convinced that normal human presence required so much restraint.

INVISIBLE IN A CROWDED ROOM

It is possible to be socially active and still feel invisible. Some people have many friends, attend events, and maintain busy lives while very few people know them deeply. They are present everywhere but revealed almost nowhere.

They may be excellent listeners. Conversations naturally turn toward the other person because they ask thoughtful questions and remember details. People leave interactions feeling understood without realizing how little they learned about the person who understood them. This can create relationships that look close from the outside but are emotionally uneven. One person is known. The other is appreciated. Those are not the same thing.

Being appreciated for what you provide in a relationship can feel good, but it cannot completely satisfy the need to be known. Sometimes they have become so practiced at directing attention away from themselves that others simply follow the direction they are given.

WHEN INVISIBILITY ENTERS YOUR WORK

The invisible self can have serious consequences professionally. Many workplaces reward not only competence but visible competence.

A highly capable person may work for years without progressing at the rate their ability would suggest, not because they lack talent but because they consistently remove themselves from the evidence of their own contribution. They wait to be discovered. They assume excellent work should speak entirely for itself. They allow more confident colleagues to dominate meetings even when they understand the subject better.

There is nothing wrong with doing excellent work without craving applause. But there is also nothing wrong with allowing accurate information about your work to exist. Visibility is not vanity. A person can communicate what they have accomplished without exaggerating it, express interest in leadership without believing themselves superior, speak with authority about something they understand without becoming arrogant. The choice is not between disappearing and becoming self important. There is a large and healthy territory between those extremes.

THE COST OF NEVER CORRECTING THE RECORD

Invisible people sometimes allow false impressions to remain because correcting them feels uncomfortable. Someone assumes they are available, so they rearrange their plans. A colleague receives disproportionate credit, and they remain silent because mentioning their own contribution feels petty.

One incident may not matter. A lifetime of them can. When you repeatedly refuse to correct inaccurate versions of yourself, you gradually begin living inside other people's interpretations.

This does not mean every misunderstanding deserves a confrontation. But there are moments when silence has a cost. If something affects your reputation, relationships, or sense of integrity, speaking may be necessary. You are allowed to say, calmly, that is not what happened. You are allowed to clarify what you meant. Being peaceful and being silent are not always the same thing.

THE ANGER OF THE UNSEEN PERSON

People who disappear for long enough sometimes develop anger that surprises everyone around them. The person who has always been agreeable suddenly becomes resentful. The employee who never complained abruptly resigns.

The invisible person may respond, how could you not know. That question deserves compassion, but it also deserves examination. Sometimes people should have known. Neglect is real. But sometimes nobody knew because the invisible person became exceptionally skilled at hiding the evidence.

This is why invisibility cannot be healed only by finding more attentive people. At some point, the unseen person must participate in becoming seen. That may mean speaking earlier, before disappointment becomes resentment, expressing a preference before everyone assumes you have none, admitting hurt instead of waiting for someone to detect it. This can feel dangerous at first. But a relationship that can survive only while you remain invisible is already costing too much.

Visibility Will Change Some Relationships

Becoming more visible does not always receive immediate applause. People who benefited from your silence may find your voice uncomfortable. Someone accustomed to making decisions for you may interpret your preferences as resistance.

This does not automatically mean they are bad people. Relationships develop expectations, and when one person changes, the system around them must adjust. Some people will adjust well. Others will resist because the earlier version of you was more convenient. This is useful information. Healing sometimes reveals which relationships loved your presence and which ones primarily loved your accommodation.

You do not need to become aggressive in response. You simply stop assuming that another person's discomfort automatically means you have done something wrong.

The Difference Between Attention and Visibility

Healing the invisible self does not mean becoming attention seeking. This distinction matters because people who have spent years avoiding attention may fear that the only alternative is becoming someone who constantly needs to be noticed.

Attention asks other people to keep looking at you. Visibility allows them to see you when seeing you is appropriate. You do not need to dominate conversations to become visible. You can listen generously and still answer honestly when someone asks about you. You can celebrate other people's accomplishments while allowing your own to be acknowledged. Visibility is not a demand to become the most important person in the room. It is the decision to stop behaving as though you are the least important.

ALLOWING GOOD THINGS TO REACH YOU

There is another side of invisibility that is easy to overlook. When we become skilled at disappearing, we do not only avoid criticism and conflict. We can also become difficult for good things to reach.

Encouragement is deflected. Praise is minimized. Opportunities are declined before they are seriously considered. Help is refused.

The protection works in both directions. If you make yourself difficult to see, painful attention may decrease, but so may healthy attention. This is one reason healing requires more than speaking up when something is wrong. It also involves learning to remain present when something good is directed toward you. When someone gives you a sincere compliment, you do not have to argue with them. When your work is recognized, you can say thank you. Receiving healthy attention may initially feel uncomfortable because discomfort often accompanies unfamiliar experiences. Unfamiliar does not mean wrong.

BECOMING VISIBLE WITHOUT BECOMING SOMEONE ELSE

The man whose director asked what he wanted did not become the loudest person in the office. He did not need to. He remained thoughtful and relatively quiet. What changed was that he stopped treating those preferences as reasons to disappear.

At the next departmental meeting, he presented an idea he had been developing instead of mentioning it privately afterward. His voice was less confident than he wanted it to be, but he finished explaining the proposal without surrendering the floor when someone interrupted.

Several weeks later, his director asked whether he wanted to lead the project. His first instinct was to say that he was happy to support whoever she selected. He recognized the sentence before it came out. Yes, he said instead. I would. The word felt strangely exposed. It also felt accurate.

At home, he began noticing smaller versions of the same pattern. When his wife asked what he wanted to do over the weekend, he stopped automatically returning the question to her. When something bothered him, he tried to mention it before the irritation had been stored for three weeks.

Not every attempt went smoothly. Years of disappearing had made visibility unfamiliar. But something important had shifted. He no longer believed that becoming visible required becoming a different personality. He was not trying to become louder. He was learning to become present.

Perhaps that is the distinction the invisible self needs most. You do not have to become impressive enough to deserve attention. You do not need to demand that every room recognize you. You do not need to abandon humility, gentleness, privacy, or a naturally quiet temperament. You simply need to stop disappearing from your own life.

There will be moments when someone else should have the floor. There will be situations where wisdom tells you that silence is better than speaking. But silence should be a choice, not an identity.

Being seen will not always feel comfortable. But there is a difference between the discomfort of becoming visible and the pain of spending an entire life unseen.

✦

SOUL MIRROR

When someone asks what you want, can you usually answer, or do you instinctively move toward what would be easiest for everyone else?

TIMELESS WISDOM

You do not have to become impressive enough to deserve attention. You only need to stop living as though your presence requires an apology.

RENEWAL PRACTICE: Practicing Healthy Visibility

For the next seven days, notice the small moments when you are tempted to erase yourself unnecessarily. Each day, record one situation in which you made yourself smaller: what happened, what you wanted to say or do, what you actually did, and what you feared might happen if you had allowed yourself to be more visible.

Then choose one ordinary act of healthy visibility to practice. State a genuine preference when someone asks. Finish your sentence after an interruption. Receive a compliment with a simple thank you instead of explaining it away. Tell someone trustworthy that something has affected you instead of hoping they will discover it indirectly.

At the end of the week, complete two sentences. I learned to become less visible because. I no longer need to disappear in order to.

Then write one final line, in your own words, about the person you are becoming.

CHAPTER TWENTY

The Self That Waits

✦

FOR ALMOST SIX years, she had been waiting to begin.

Not literally. She went to work, paid bills, remembered birthdays, attended weddings, took holidays, laughed with friends, and did all the ordinary things that made her life look full from the outside.

But somewhere inside, her real life was always scheduled for later.

She would feel better about herself when she lost the weight. She would travel when she had someone to travel with. She would apply for the position when she felt more qualified. She would buy clothes she really liked when her body looked different. She would become more confident when she had achieved something worth being confident about.

There was always a condition standing between her and permission to fully inhabit her own life.

Then one evening, while sorting through photographs on her phone, she found a picture taken five years earlier. She remembered disliking it at the time. She had thought she looked too heavy, too tired, not quite put together enough.

Looking at it now, she saw something completely different. She looked young. Happy, actually. There was sunlight behind her, and she was laughing at whoever had taken the photograph.

She stared at the woman she had once considered not good enough and felt something unexpectedly close to grief.

She had spent five years waiting to become acceptable to herself. And the woman in the photograph had already been living.

When Life Becomes Conditional

There is nothing wrong with wanting your life to improve. Goals matter. Growth matters. Becoming healthier, developing a career, building financial stability, repairing a relationship, or learning something new can all be worthwhile pursuits.

The problem begins when improvement becomes the price of admission to your own life. I will be worthy when. I will be happy when. I will finally feel like myself when. That little word when can quietly hold an entire identity hostage.

The self that waits is not necessarily lazy or unmotivated. Often it is the opposite, working extremely hard. What makes it different is the belief underneath the work, that the person you are today is somehow provisional. Not quite the finished version. The version that deserves love, confidence, enjoyment, or rest is still somewhere ahead. So today becomes a waiting room, and tomorrow keeps moving.

The Future Self

Most of us carry some picture of who we hope to become, and there is nothing unhealthy about that. Human beings need imagination. We need to be able to see possibilities beyond our present circumstances.

But there is a difference between having a future self and rejecting your present one. The future self says, I am growing. The waiting self says, I am not enough yet.

That distinction matters more than it sounds like it should, because the second belief has a way of outlasting almost anything you throw at it. You have likely already watched it happen in your own life, a goal reached, and the satisfaction lasting a week before a new, better version of the same goal takes its place. The finish line was never really the problem this book has been pointing at all along. The problem was always the belief that something outside you would eventually settle something inside you, and that belief does not check whether the goal was actually met before finding its next assignment.

Being Behind, Revisited

There is a particular version of waiting worth naming here, though this book has already spent real time on it. Waiting to catch up. An age by which certain things were supposed to have happened, and the quiet conversion of timing into identity. I am behind.

The fuller treatment of that question, and of who actually gets to set the timeline you are measuring yourself against, is already sitting in this book's chapter on culture. What is worth adding here is simply this: being behind and being unworthy are two different conclusions from the same delayed dream, and the self that waits has a habit of quietly swapping one for the other without ever checking whether the swap was justified.

Waiting for Someone to Choose You

The text arrived on a Tuesday, after five weeks of nothing. Hey stranger, miss you, we should catch up sometime.

She read it standing in her kitchen and felt her whole week quietly reorganize itself around four words at the end of a sentence, sometime, no date attached, no plan behind it, and still enough to make her cancel a Thursday dinner with a friend on the chance he might actually follow through. He rarely did. Three years of this now, an easy warmth whenever he resurfaced, long stretches of silence in between, and never once anything that looked like an actual relationship, though she had turned down two men in that time who had been entirely straightforward about wanting one.

She did not think of herself as waiting for him, exactly. If asked, she would have said she was simply not in a rush, that things happened when they were supposed to happen. But she had noticed, in a detached sort of way, that she kept a certain amount of herself unspent, available, on the chance that this particular Tuesday text might finally be the one that turned into something. It rarely was. It had never once been.

There is another kind of waiting that can reach particularly deep. Waiting to be chosen. For the relationship. For the friendship. For somebody to notice what you can do. For the person who keeps giving you just enough attention to make you believe that one day they may finally give you more.

Waiting can begin to organize a life. You stay emotionally available to someone who has never actually made themselves available to you. You keep a door open because closing it would mean admitting that what you hoped for may not happen. You hesitate to move forward because some part of you is still listening for footsteps behind you.

Hope is not foolish. But hope needs evidence. There comes a point when waiting for someone else to decide your value becomes another way of handing them authority over it. Being chosen can be beautiful. It should never be the event that proves you were worth choosing.

THE LIFE YOU KEEP POSTPONING

One of the saddest things about conditional living is that the conditions often look reasonable. When work settles down. When the children are older. When I have more money. When I feel confident. When somebody comes with me.

Some of those reasons are real. Life has seasons, responsibilities, and limits. Not everything can happen now. But sometimes not now becomes a habit long after the original reason has disappeared. You stop asking whether you could do something and automatically assume it belongs to a later version of your life.

There are clothes waiting for a different body. Ideas waiting for more confidence. Conversations waiting for courage. Rest waiting until everything is finished. Joy waiting until something improves. And because life rarely becomes completely settled, the permission never arrives.

YOU DO NOT HAVE TO EARN THE PRESENT

Growth does not require contempt for the person who has not finished growing.

You can want to become healthier and still respect the body carrying you today. You can want a better career without treating your present work as proof that you failed. You can desire marriage without considering singleness an unfinished identity. You can recognize what needs changing without turning yourself into a problem that must be solved before life can begin.

This is not settling. Settling says nothing needs to change. Self acceptance says change is allowed to happen without hatred being its fuel. That is a very different thing. The person you hope to become does not need you to despise the person doing the becoming.

BEGIN FROM HERE

There is probably something you are waiting for. Maybe it should be waited for. Wisdom includes timing.

But perhaps there is also something you have postponed unnecessarily because you attached permission to a condition that was never actually required. You do not need complete confidence before taking one brave step. You do not need another person's company before enjoying your own. You do not need the perfect body before appearing in photographs. You do not need to have arrived before you are allowed to live like someone whose life already matters.

Your future deserves attention. So does today. The person you are becoming is important. But the person reading this sentence is already here.

Do not spend so much of your life waiting for yourself, or waiting for someone else to finally arrive at a decision they were never actually working toward, that you miss the self who has been living it all along.

✦

SOUL MIRROR

What have you been telling yourself you are not allowed to fully enjoy, attempt, or become until something else happens first?

TIMELESS WISDOM

Growth asks you to move forward. Shame tells you that you are not allowed to belong where you are. Learn the difference.

RENEWAL PRACTICE: The Permission List

Write this sentence at the top of a page. I will finally ______ when ______.

Complete it five times without trying to make the answers impressive. Then look carefully at the condition in the second blank. For each one, ask whether this condition is genuinely necessary, what you are afraid would happen if you stopped waiting, and what small part of this you could begin now.

Choose one. Not the largest. Not the most dramatic. One thing you have been unnecessarily postponing. Do something small this week that belongs to the life you keep telling yourself will begin later.

Let yourself discover that some doors were never locked. You were simply waiting for permission.

CHAPTER TWENTY-ONE

The Stories We Tell Ourselves

✦

THE EMAIL WAS shorter than she expected.

She had interviewed twice for the position and had left the second interview feeling unusually hopeful. The conversation had gone well. They had asked when she could start, discussed the team she would supervise, and introduced her to two people she would be working with. For several days, she allowed herself to imagine what accepting the job might change.

Then the email arrived.

They had chosen another candidate.

She read it once, then again, as though a second reading might reveal something the first had missed. There was nothing unusual in the message. They thanked her for her time, said the decision had been difficult, and wished her well.

The facts were simple. She applied. She interviewed. Someone else was selected.

But within minutes, the facts had acquired a story.

She had probably embarrassed herself by being too confident in the interview. They must have realized she was not as qualified as she appeared on paper. Perhaps she had been foolish to think she was ready for that level of responsibility. She remembered another promotion she had missed three years earlier and connected the two events almost immediately.

Maybe this was simply where she belonged.

By the end of the evening, one unsuccessful application had become evidence about her career, her ability, and eventually herself.

Nothing in the email had said any of those things. She had supplied the rest.

WHAT HAPPENED AND WHAT IT MEANT

Human beings do more than experience events. We interpret them.

Something happens, and almost immediately the mind begins trying to understand what it means. Why did this happen. What does it say about me. What should I expect next. Have I seen this before.

This ability is necessary. Without interpretation, life would be a collection of disconnected events from which we learned very little. The difficulty is that conclusions are not always facts.

A friend fails to return your call. That is an event. She is upset with me is an interpretation.

Your marriage ends. That is an event. I am impossible to love is an interpretation.

You make a poor financial decision. That is an event. I always ruin everything is an interpretation.

Sometimes our interpretation is accurate. The friend may actually be upset. The criticism may identify something that needs improvement. The problem begins when we stop recognizing that an interpretation has taken place. The story becomes so familiar that it starts sounding like the event itself.

HOW ONE MOMENT BECOMES A PATTERN

Most identity stories are not built from one event alone. They become convincing because the mind begins collecting similar experiences.

A child struggles in mathematics and feels embarrassed when asked to solve a problem in front of the class. A few months later, a teacher comments that the child is stronger in creative subjects. Later still, a sibling performs better academically. None of these moments independently proves anything about the child's overall intelligence. But the child may connect them into a story: I am not smart.

Once that story exists, new experiences are interpreted through it. A poor grade fits the story perfectly. A good grade may be dismissed as an easy test. This is how stories become powerful. They do not merely explain the past. They begin organizing what we notice in the present.

If your story is people eventually leave, every departure carries unusual significance. If your story is nothing ever works out for me, disappointment becomes memorable while ordinary successes are treated as exceptions. The story begins selecting its own evidence.

That does not mean you are deliberately deceiving yourself. Most of this happens quietly. The danger is that a story can become stronger simply because we have been telling it for a long time.

The Words That Make a Story Permanent

Certain words should make us pay attention when they appear in our private descriptions of ourselves. Always. Never. Everyone. No one. Every time. Nothing.

I always mess things up. Nobody ever stays. People never take me seriously. Every time I trust someone, I regret it.

These words turn experiences into laws. Sometimes they emerge from genuine frustration, and we do not need to police every exaggerated sentence we say after a difficult day. But when the same language appears repeatedly, it is worth examining.

Perhaps you have made several poor relationship choices. That deserves reflection. It is still different from I will always choose the wrong person. Perhaps you have failed at something more than once. That may tell you your approach needs to change. It does not automatically tell you what you are capable of becoming.

A story becomes particularly restrictive when it takes something that happened repeatedly and turns it into something that must happen permanently. History deserves to inform us. It does not automatically deserve to predict us.

THE STORY BEHIND THE REACTION

Sometimes the easiest way to discover an internal story is to pay attention to reactions that seem larger than the immediate event.

Imagine that two employees receive the same constructive criticism from a supervisor. One hears useful information, thinks about it, and moves on. The other spends the rest of the day distressed, and by evening the criticism has become evidence that the supervisor regrets hiring them.

The difference may not be the criticism. It may be the story the criticism entered. If someone already carries a story that says I am one mistake away from being exposed, ordinary correction can feel like confirmation.

Instead of asking only, why did this bother me so much, it can be useful to ask, what did this seem to prove. The answer often takes us closer to the real issue.

STORIES WE INHERIT

Not every story about ourselves begins with us.

Families tell stories about their members, sometimes so consistently that the description becomes part of how everyone understands the person. Earlier in this book, we examined the identities we inherit and the roles families assign. Those family messages can continue inside us long after nobody is actively repeating them. The difficult one. The clever one. The one who can handle everything.

Even positive stories can become restrictive when they leave no room for change. Culture contributes stories too, about what a successful life should look like and what should have happened by a certain age.

The important question is not whether other people influenced your story. Of course they did. The question is whether every part of the story still deserves your agreement.

The Story That Protects You

Some stories survive because they protect us from disappointment.

Consider the person who repeatedly says, I don't really care about relationships. Perhaps that is true. But sometimes the fuller story is different. They cared deeply once. They were rejected, and deciding that relationships did not matter became less painful than continuing to want one.

A story can reduce pain by reducing expectation. If I convince myself I never wanted it, I do not have to grieve not having it. These stories can feel like self knowledge because we have lived with them for so long. Sometimes they are actually old protection wearing the language of personality.

When the Story Becomes an Excuse

Not every limiting story makes us feel bad about ourselves. Some stories protect us from responsibility.

This is just how I am. I've always had a temper. I don't do commitment.

A story can become an explanation that quietly removes the expectation of change. There is relief in having a reason for our behavior, and understanding where a pattern came from is valuable. But explanation and permission are not the same thing.

Your history may explain why you avoid difficult conversations. It does not mean everyone around you must live indefinitely with the consequences. Understanding should increase our ability to choose. If it only gives us a more sophisticated reason to remain exactly the same, we have stopped using the story to understand ourselves and started using it to protect ourselves from growth.

The Problem With a Single Story

No human life can be explained accurately by one sentence.

You may have failed, but you have also learned. You may have been rejected, but you have also been welcomed. This does not mean balancing every painful truth with forced positivity. The goal is accuracy, not optimism.

If you have repeatedly behaved irresponsibly, the answer is not to tell yourself you are secretly responsible. It is to acknowledge the pattern honestly while refusing to make the pattern your entire identity. A fuller story might be: I have handled money poorly in the past, and I am learning to handle it differently. Notice what that does. It tells the truth about the past without using the past to close the future.

Memory Is Not a Courtroom Transcript

We often treat memory as though it were a perfect recording of what happened. It is not.

We remember real events, but memory is selective. Certain moments remain vivid because they carried strong emotion. Over the years, we may remember the experiences that support an established story more easily than experiences that challenge it.

A person who believes they were always excluded may vividly remember the birthday party they were not invited to at fourteen while barely remembering the classmates who regularly included them. This does not mean the painful memories are false. It means memory alone may not tell the entire story.

Sometimes healing requires allowing additional evidence into the record. Who did believe in you. When did you cope better than you remember. Where did you make a good decision. These questions do not erase painful evidence. They prevent painful evidence from becoming the only evidence admitted.

Other People's Outdated Version of You

We already looked at how a family can keep interacting with a version of someone that stopped existing years ago. The same thing happens with stories specifically, not just roles. A family member still treats you as irresponsible because you were careless at twenty, though you have spent fifteen years building a stable life. Someone remembers a mistake long after you have repaired what you could and changed the behavior that caused it.

Other people's stories can be surprisingly difficult to escape because familiarity gives them emotional authority. You may find yourself returning to an old version of yourself around people who knew you then.

You cannot force everyone to revise their story about you. Some will. Some will not. Your responsibility is to make sure you are not continuing to live according to a version of yourself that is no longer accurate simply because somebody else has not noticed the change.

A Better Story Is Not a Prettier Story

There is a temptation in personal growth to replace painful stories with flattering ones. I was never the problem. Everything happened for a reason. I can do anything I decide to do.

These statements may feel empowering, but empowerment built on distortion is fragile. Renewal does not require turning yourself into the hero of every story. Sometimes you were wrong. Sometimes another person was right about something you did not want to hear.

A healthier story can contain responsibility without becoming condemnation. It can say, I did something I regret, and I have learned from it. Truth does not need to flatter you in order to free you. It simply needs to be more complete than the story that has been controlling you.

Returning to the Email

Several days after receiving the rejection, the woman who had begun questioning her entire career called someone she trusted professionally.

She expected encouragement. Instead, her former supervisor asked her a simple question.

What exactly did they say?

She explained the interviews and read the rejection email aloud.

And where, he asked, did they say you weren't capable of doing the job?

She became irritated. They didn't have to say it. They chose somebody else.

That tells you who they chose. It doesn't tell you everything you are making it tell you.

The distinction stayed with her. She had taken one fact and built an entire explanation around it. Perhaps the other candidate had more experience. She did not know. What she did know was that the rejection had immediately attached itself to an older story: I am not quite ready for the next level.

That story had influenced her before. It had made her delay applications until she met nearly every requirement. It had kept her waiting for confidence before attempting things that might actually have built confidence.

The rejection still disappointed her. Examining the story did not make the outcome pleasant. But it returned the event to its proper size. She had applied for a job and had not been selected. That was painful. It was also all she actually knew.

A month later, another position opened. She noticed the old story immediately, explaining why she should wait, gain another year of experience, and avoid another disappointment.

This time she recognized the voice without automatically obeying it.

She applied. Not because she had replaced the old story with certainty that she would succeed, but because she had stopped treating uncertainty as proof that she should not try.

For years, she had assumed the story in her head was simply an accurate description of her life. Now she understood that a story could contain pieces of truth and still reach the wrong conclusion.

The events of her life mattered. So did the meaning she gave them. And for the first time, she realized that meaning could be examined before it became identity.

✦

SOUL MIRROR

Think of one sentence you repeat about yourself often enough that it now feels like a fact. Does it describe something that has happened, or has it quietly become a prediction about what must always happen?

TIMELESS WISDOM

An event can be true while the story you built around it is incomplete. You do not need to deny your history to examine its meaning.

RENEWAL PRACTICE: Fact, Story, Fuller Truth

Choose one situation that still affects how you see yourself. Divide a page into three sections.

In the first, write what happened. Describe only the facts, removing assumptions about motives and conclusions about your worth.

In the second, write the story you told yourself. Record what you concluded because of the event, and be honest about words like always, never, nobody, and everyone.

In the third, write the fuller truth. Not a positive slogan, something you can genuinely defend. Perhaps: I was rejected by someone I loved, and that hurt deeply. It does not establish that everyone I love will eventually reject me.

The first tells you what happened. The second shows you what you made it mean. The third gives you somewhere more truthful to live.

You cannot rewrite every event in your story. You can become more careful about what you allow those events to say about who you are.

CHAPTER TWENTY-TWO

Shame: When Failure Becomes Identity

✦

HE HAD NOT told anyone about the debt.

His wife knew that money was tight, but she did not know how tight. She knew the business had struggled during the previous year, but she did not know that he had used personal credit to keep it operating or that several payments were now overdue. Every month he became more creative about moving money from one place to another, convincing himself that one good contract would allow him to put everything right.

The contract never came.

By the time the truth could no longer be hidden, the financial problem was serious. His wife sat across from him at the kitchen table with statements spread between them and asked the question he had been dreading.

Why didn't you tell me?

He had prepared explanations about cash flow, clients who paid late, unexpected expenses, and decisions that had seemed reasonable at the time. All of those things were true.

But they were not the real answer.

I was ashamed.

He had always thought of himself as responsible. He was the person who understood money, solved problems, and protected his family from unnecessary worry. Admitting that some of his own decisions had made the situation worse felt unbearable.

So he hid the problem until hiding it created another problem.

The debt was serious, but something deeper had happened before the numbers became impossible. Somewhere along the way, he had stopped thinking, I have made mistakes, and started thinking, I am a failure.

Once that happened, telling the truth no longer felt like revealing a problem. It felt like revealing himself.

FROM BEHAVIOR TO IDENTITY

We already spent real time in this book on the gap between correcting what someone did and condemning who they are. Shame is what happens when that gap collapses from the inside, without anyone else needing to say a word. I did something wrong becomes there is something wrong with me, quietly and almost immediately, and once the collapse happens, examining what actually went wrong starts to feel like an attack on the self rather than useful information.

You can know intellectually that everyone makes mistakes and still experience your own mistake as evidence of something deeply defective. You can offer a friend compassion for the exact decision you cannot forgive in yourself. That asymmetry is shame's signature, and it is worth naming before going further into how it actually operates.

GUILT AND SHAME ARE NOT THE SAME THING

Guilt and shame often appear together, but they do different work.

Healthy guilt tells us that something needs attention. We acted against our values, hurt someone, or failed to keep a commitment. That discomfort can be useful. It can lead us to apologize, repair damage where possible, or make a different decision next time.

Shame goes further. Instead of saying, that action was wrong, shame says, you are what is wrong. This difference matters because responsibility requires enough separation between the person and the behavior for the behavior to be examined honestly. If every mistake becomes proof that you are fundamentally defective, you may become more interested in escaping exposure than correcting what happened. That is why shame, despite feeling morally serious, can actually interfere with responsibility.

A person who can say, I lied, and I need to understand why I did that, has somewhere to go. A person who can only say, I am horrible, may remain trapped in self condemnation without ever addressing the pattern that produced the lie. Feeling worse about yourself is not the same as becoming better.

WHY SHAME WANTS SECRECY

Shame rarely wants witnesses. It tells us that if people knew the whole truth, their opinion of us would change permanently, that they would lose respect or withdraw affection, perhaps confirming the judgment we have already made about ourselves.

So we hide. We hide financial problems, addictions, failures, relationship difficulties, and sometimes ordinary human weaknesses that would not shock anyone nearly as much as we imagine. The hiding creates temporary relief because what is concealed cannot immediately be judged. But secrecy also gives shame unusual freedom. When nobody trustworthy knows what happened, nobody can challenge the conclusions we are drawing from it. We become prosecutor, witness, judge, and jury, and the verdict is rarely gentle.

This was what happened to the man with the failing business. He was not only hiding debt. He was protecting an identity. He wanted his wife to continue seeing the competent man he was afraid he no longer was. The irony was that protecting that image required behavior increasingly inconsistent with the person he wanted to be. Shame often creates exactly this contradiction. We hide because we are afraid the truth will damage our identity, and the hiding begins damaging our character.

The Shame of Things You Did Not Choose

Not all shame comes from something we did wrong, and this is one of the most important distinctions in any honest discussion of shame.

People can feel ashamed of things that were done to them. A child may carry shame after abuse even though the child was not responsible. A person who grew up in poverty may feel ashamed of where they lived or what their family could not afford. People experience shame around infertility, divorce, illness, unemployment, and countless other circumstances that cannot reasonably be reduced to personal wrongdoing.

Shame does not always ask whether you were responsible. It asks whether the experience made you feel exposed, diminished, or different from the people around you. That is why people sometimes hide things for which they have nothing to apologize. The emotional message is not necessarily I did wrong. Sometimes it is simply I do not want anyone to know this is part of my life. This kind of shame requires a different response from guilt. There may be nothing to confess and nothing to repair. What needs to change is the belief that an experience you did not choose has somehow reduced your human worth.

Public Failure and the Loss of the Old Self

Some failures hurt more because other people witnessed them. A private mistake can sometimes be corrected quietly. Public failure changes the social environment around the experience.

Part of the pain comes from the failure itself. Another part comes from knowing that other people now possess information you would rather they did not have. You begin imagining conversations that may or may not be happening. What do they think of me now. Did they always know I wasn't capable.

This is especially difficult when we had become identified with the opposite of what happened. The successful person fails. The financially responsible person goes bankrupt. The event does not merely hurt. It contradicts the version of ourselves we were accustomed to presenting. That contradiction can become an invitation to a more honest identity, but it rarely feels like one at first. At first, it simply feels like exposure.

PERFECTION AS A SHIELD

We already looked, in an earlier chapter, at what happens when achievement becomes a performance rather than a pursuit. There is a shame specific version of that same pattern worth naming here.

If I never make the mistake, nobody can see that I am inadequate. If my home, career, and relationships look successful, perhaps nobody will see the parts of me I am afraid would not survive inspection. Perfection cannot provide lasting protection, because human beings eventually make mistakes regardless of how carefully they prepare. If identity depends on preventing all exposure, ordinary human imperfection becomes an ongoing threat. The healthier alternative is not lowering every standard. It is developing a self that can survive being imperfect in public.

SHAME AFTER SUCCESS

Shame is not limited to people whose lives are visibly falling apart. Sometimes it becomes stronger after success.

A person who has built a respected career may feel even more pressure to hide an area of struggle because there is now more reputation to protect. Success can increase the distance between the public self and the private struggle, and the wider that distance becomes, the lonelier a person may feel. Everyone praises the version they can see while the person privately wonders what would happen if they saw the rest.

This is one reason external admiration cannot cure shame. You can receive praise all day and still believe the praise belongs only to the version of you that has been successfully presented. Shame says, they like what they know, if they knew everything, they would think differently. Healing begins when worth no longer depends upon maintaining a flawless presentation.

WHEN SHAME MAKES US DEFENSIVE

Shame does not always look like hiding. Sometimes it looks like anger.

A person is confronted about something they did, and instead of listening, they immediately explain why the other person is also wrong, shift the conversation, or bring up an old offense. This can appear arrogant, but underneath the defensiveness there may be a person who does not know how to be wrong without becoming worthless.

This is why a secure identity makes accountability easier rather than harder. When I know that one failure does not contain the whole truth about me, I can look at the failure more directly. I can say, I was wrong. I can apologize without spending half the apology defending my intentions. Shame tells us that self condemnation proves we understand the seriousness of what happened. It does not. Sometimes the most responsible thing a person can do is refuse to spend all their energy hating themselves and use that energy to repair what can actually be repaired.

THE PUNISHMENT THAT NEVER ENDS

There are people who have taken responsibility for something, apologized, changed their behavior, and still believe they are not allowed to move forward. They continue punishing themselves long after the punishment has stopped serving any useful purpose, refusing opportunities because they do not feel deserving, or sabotaging healthy relationships because someone better should have them.

This can feel like humility. It is not. There is no moral value in remaining permanently chained to a version of yourself you have already confronted and changed.

Consequences may remain. Forgiveness does not erase every consequence or require other people to trust immediately. But consequences and identity are still different. You may need to live responsibly with what happened without living forever as though nothing else about you is allowed to become true. A mistake can become part of your history without remaining your permanent address.

WHEN OTHER PEOPLE KEEP YOU IN SHAME

Sometimes the person struggling to move beyond failure is not the only one keeping it alive. Families, partners, and communities can do this too. You may have apologized and changed, but every disagreement returns to the same old mistake, as though no amount of present growth is allowed to outweigh the past.

Accountability and permanent humiliation are not the same thing. Trust may need rebuilding, and you do not get to decide how quickly someone else should recover. But there is a difference between allowing consequences and accepting an identity assigned by someone who refuses to let you become more than your worst moment. You can acknowledge what you did without agreeing that it is all you are. Other people are entitled to their memory of what happened. They are not entitled to permanent ownership of your identity.

TELLING THE TRUTH WITHOUT BECOMING THE TRUTH

The way out of shame is not denial. It is truth told at the correct size.

I failed. I lied. I stayed when I should have left. I hurt someone. I was afraid.

These statements may be painful, but they are specific. Shame prefers larger language. I am a failure. I destroy relationships. I am disgraceful. Specific truth creates somewhere to work. Global condemnation does not. If you made a destructive decision, you can examine the decision. If you harmed someone, you can consider repair. But if the entire self has become the problem, where exactly do you begin.

You are not avoiding responsibility when you describe what happened accurately. You are making responsibility possible.

BACK AT THE KITCHEN TABLE

The conversation about the debt lasted much longer than the man expected.

His wife was angry. She had every right to be. What hurt her most was not only the money. It was that he had decided, without consulting her, that she could not handle the truth. In trying to protect her from worry and himself from embarrassment, he had removed her from decisions that affected both of them.

There was no quick resolution. They had to meet with a financial adviser. Some plans were postponed. He closed the business several months later, an outcome he had spent more than a year trying to prevent.

For a while, closing it felt like confirmation of everything he had feared.

Then life continued. His wife was disappointed in some of his decisions, but she did not stop loving him. A few people knew the business had failed, and most of them moved on with their own lives far more quickly than he had imagined. He found other work. They paid down the debt slowly.

The most difficult work was quieter. He had to learn to describe the experience without turning it into a description of himself. The business failed. Some circumstances were outside his control. Some decisions were not. He had hidden things he should have disclosed. He regretted that. He had learned from it. All of those sentences could be true at the same time.

Years later, he could talk about the business without immediately trying to explain why the failure was not really his fault and without using it as evidence that he should never take another meaningful risk. The memory still carried regret. What it no longer carried was a verdict.

There is a difference between having a scar and having an open wound. Both tell you that something happened, but only one requires your life to keep organizing itself around the injury.

Shame had spent years telling him that if the truth came fully into the light, he would become smaller in the eyes of everyone who mattered. The truth did cost him something. But it also gave him something shame never could. The ability to be known without pretending he had never failed.

✦

SOUL MIRROR

Think of something in your life that is difficult to discuss because it carries shame. When you think about it, do you describe something that happened, or something you believe you are?

TIMELESS WISDOM

You can take responsibility without becoming the mistake. The most honest sentence is neither I did nothing wrong nor I am terrible, but something more mature: this happened, this part belongs to me, and I refuse to make it the whole definition of who I am.

RENEWAL PRACTICE: From Verdict to Truth

Choose one experience that still carries shame. Write the sentence you normally use internally when you think about it, and notice the identity language in it, especially anything beginning with I am.

Rewrite it using specific language about what actually happened. Instead of I am a failure, write what failed. Instead of I ruin relationships, identify what you did that you regret.

Then divide responsibility honestly into two lists. What belongs to me: your own decisions and actions, without excuses. What does not belong to me: another person's choices, or circumstances you could not control.

Finally, write what you can do now. There may be an apology to make, a pattern to change, or a consequence to accept. There may also be nothing left to repair, in which case your work is simply learning to stop reopening a case that has already taught you what it had to teach.

You are not trying to make the past disappear. You are putting it back where it belongs, in your history, where it can inform you without becoming your identity.

CHAPTER TWENTY-THREE

Separating Who You Are From What Happened to You

✦

FOR TWENTY TWO years, she had been married.

Then she wasn't.

The change took less time to say than it took to understand. There were documents to sign, accounts to separate, belongings to divide, people to tell. Friends who had known them as a couple for years struggled to know what to say. Invitations changed. Weekends changed. Holidays changed. Even ordinary introductions felt different.

For the first few months, she answered questions by explaining what had happened.

How are you? Going through a divorce. What have you been doing lately? Trying to get through the divorce. Are you coming for Christmas? I'm not sure. Everything is complicated because of the divorce.

This was understandable. The experience was enormous. But eventually she noticed something. The divorce had become the first fact she knew about herself. She was no longer simply a woman who had experienced the end of a marriage. She had begun seeing herself primarily as a divorced woman, and from that position she was quietly reconsidering everything else. Was she still someone who understood relationships. Had twenty two years become evidence of poor judgment because the marriage had ended.

One evening, a longtime friend said something that irritated her.

This happened to your life. It didn't become your life.

She did not appreciate the distinction immediately. Months later, she would.

THE DIFFERENCE BETWEEN AN EXPERIENCE AND AN IDENTITY

Life gives us many descriptions. Married. Divorced. Employed. Healthy. Ill. Parent. Widow. Bankrupt. Some last for decades. Others change within a year. Some are chosen. Others arrive without permission.

They matter because circumstances affect us. Losing a job can change finances, confidence, and relationships. Illness can alter what a person is physically able to do. There is no wisdom in pretending these experiences are merely labels with no emotional weight.

But there is an equally important truth. A description of your circumstances is not a complete description of you. Something can become deeply important without becoming total. This distinction is easy to understand when life is going well. It becomes much harder when one event becomes large enough to dominate almost everything else.

WHEN ONE THING TAKES UP THE WHOLE ROOM

Certain experiences are so consuming that it is natural for them to occupy most of our attention for a while. A new parent may spend months thinking almost entirely about the baby. Someone grieving a death may find that grief enters every part of the day. There is nothing unhealthy about allowing a significant experience to be significant.

The problem begins when temporary emotional dominance becomes permanent identity. You stop saying, I lost my job, and begin living as though unemployment has revealed your actual value. You stop saying, my relationship ended, and begin assuming the ending has told you something final about your ability to be loved. The event expands until everything else about you seems smaller beside it.

This is especially likely when the experience disrupts something that previously gave life structure. The question is no longer only, what happened. It becomes, who am I now.

WHAT CHANGED AND WHAT DID NOT

After a major life event, it can feel as though everything has changed. Usually, everything has not.

A man who loses a business may lose income, status, and plans he had spent years building. Those losses are real. But perhaps he is still disciplined, still a father, still capable of learning, still someone who has survived difficult seasons before.

One useful question during major change is very simple. What changed, and what did not. The first part allows grief. The second protects identity. We need both. If we focus only on what remains, we may rush ourselves past legitimate loss. If we focus only on what disappeared, we may begin believing that we disappeared with it.

YOU WERE A PERSON BEFORE THE ROLE

This book has already spent real time on what happens when a defining role ends, at retirement, when the last child leaves, when a caregiving season closes. The same mechanism belongs here too, stated plainly rather than retold. Before you became someone's spouse, parent, caregiver, or employee, there was a person capable of entering that role. When the role changes, that person does not cease to exist. You may simply need time to meet them again, because even the most meaningful role is something you occupy. It was never the entirety of the person occupying it.

THE DANGER OF BECOMING THE DIAGNOSIS

There are experiences in which language is genuinely useful because naming something helps us understand what is happening. A diagnosis can bring relief after years of unexplained symptoms. It can provide access to treatment and appropriate expectations.

But even useful language can become too large. There is a difference between having a condition and allowing the condition to become the first and most important answer to who you are. This applies beyond physical or mental health. People can become identified with infertility, addiction recovery, disability, or financial hardship, or any experience that requires sustained attention. The issue is not whether the description is accurate. It may be completely accurate. The issue is proportion. You are allowed to take something seriously without allowing it to consume every other truth about you. A diagnosis may explain something about your body or mind. It does not contain your entire biography.

WHEN OTHER PEOPLE KEEP INTRODUCING YOU BY IT

This book has already looked, more than once, at what happens when the people around you keep interacting with a version of you that no longer exists. The same thing happens through introductions specifically. She is the one whose husband left. He is the man who lost his company. The descriptions are rarely malicious. People naturally use memorable information to locate one another socially.

What is worth adding here is simply this. You may have done considerable work to rebuild your life while other people continue relating to you as though you are still standing in the worst year of it. There is real freedom in realizing that other people's descriptions do not have to become your internal language. They may remember the event first. You do not have to.

WHEN SOMETHING GOOD BECOMES IDENTITY

We usually notice identity problems more easily when the experience is painful. But this book has already shown, in its own dedicated territory, how positive experiences, appearance, success, achievement, can take over identity just as completely, and become just as frightening to lose.

What is worth naming here is the general principle underneath all of those specific cases. Separating identity from experience is not simply a recovery skill for people going through difficult circumstances. It is a way of living. Enjoy what is good. Grieve what is lost. Learn from what is painful. But be careful about asking any circumstance, pleasant or painful, to carry the full weight of your identity. Life changes too much for that.

THE LANGUAGE OF "I AM"

Words do not create reality simply because we say them, but language reveals how we are organizing reality internally.

Notice what follows the words I am. I am divorced. I am broke. I am sick. I am unemployed. These statements may be factually correct in ordinary conversation, and there is no need to become unnatural about language. But internally, it can help to become more precise. I am going through a divorce. I am experiencing financial difficulty. I am living with an illness. I feel alone in this season.

The difference may appear small, but psychologically it creates space between the person and the circumstance. One describes identity. The other describes experience. Sometimes that small space is exactly where hope begins.

YOU ARE ALLOWED TO OUTGROW AN OLD DESCRIPTION

Some experiences continue shaping identity long after the circumstances have changed. The child who grew up poor becomes financially secure but still thinks of herself as the poor girl who somehow got lucky. The person who struggled academically decades ago continues saying, I'm not very smart, despite years of evidence showing competence.

We can become loyal to old descriptions because they are familiar. Change creates a strange problem. The evidence may have changed before identity catches up. You may already be living differently while still describing yourself according to an earlier version of your life. At some point, accuracy requires updating the language. This is not pretending the past did not happen. It is refusing to freeze yourself there.

SOME EXPERIENCES WILL ALWAYS MATTER

Separating yourself from what happened does not mean reaching a point where important experiences no longer matter. Some things become permanent parts of our story. A parent who loses a child does not need to stop being affected by that loss in order to be healthy. A betrayal may permanently change how someone approaches trust.

Integration is not erasure. The goal is not to become the person you would have been if nothing difficult had ever happened. That person does not exist. The goal is to become someone who can carry the experience without requiring the experience to carry the entire identity. You can be changed by something without being reduced to it.

WHAT REMAINS WHEN THE CHAPTER CHANGES

The woman whose marriage ended eventually moved into a smaller home.

At first, almost everything about the house felt like evidence of loss. Half the closet space. A smaller dining table. A different neighborhood. Boxes containing things she had not yet decided whether to keep.

One Saturday morning, nearly a year after the separation, she found herself sitting on the floor sorting through photographs. There were wedding pictures, holidays, children's birthdays, ordinary afternoons she had forgotten anyone photographed. Her first instinct was to divide the pictures mentally into before and after.

Then she noticed herself in one photograph taken many years earlier. She was laughing with her sister. Her husband was not in the picture. She looked at another. She was holding her newborn daughter. Another showed her graduating. Another showed her standing beside her mother.

It occurred to her that the marriage had been a significant part of her story, but it had never been the only story happening. She had been a daughter while she was a wife. A mother. A sister. A friend. A professional. A woman with interests, opinions, gifts, and hopes that did not begin on her wedding day and did not disappear when the marriage ended.

This did not suddenly make the divorce easy. There were things she still grieved. There were parts of the future she had expected to share with someone that she now had to imagine differently. But the friend who had irritated her months earlier had been right. Something enormous had happened to her life. It had not become the whole of her life.

She stopped trying to become the woman she had been before the divorce. Too much had changed for that. Instead, she became curious about the woman who remained. Not the divorced woman. Not the abandoned woman. Simply the woman who had lived through all of it and was still here.

Perhaps identity renewal sometimes begins there. Not by denying what happened. Not by rushing to make meaning from it. But by recognizing that even after an experience changes the shape of your life, there is still a person standing inside that changed life who deserves to be known as more than what happened.

✦

SOUL MIRROR

Think of one experience, role, or season that has become strongly attached to how you describe yourself. What did it change? Now ask the question we often forget: what did it not change?

TIMELESS WISDOM

What happened to you may explain part of your story without becoming the definition of the person who lived it. Some chapters change everything that comes afterward. They still do not become the whole book.

RENEWAL PRACTICE: What Changed, What Remained

Choose one significant experience that changed how you see yourself. Divide a page into two columns.

In the first, write what changed. Be honest about the practical and emotional consequences. Do not minimize what was lost.

In the second, write what remained. This column may be harder. Do not list possessions or circumstances. Look for qualities, values, abilities, relationships, and parts of yourself the experience did not remove.

Then write one sentence describing the experience without turning it into an identity. Instead of I am a failure, write something I worked hard to build did not succeed. Instead of I am abandoned, write someone I loved chose to leave, and I am learning how to live after that loss. Do not force the sentence to sound positive. Make it accurate.

Honor what changed. Grieve what needs grieving. But pay attention to what remained.

You are not only the person something happened to. You are also the person who remains after it happened. And that person is still becoming.

CHAPTER TWENTY-FOUR

Questioning the Voices Within

✦

SHE HAD BEEN invited to speak at a professional conference for the first time.

The invitation should have felt like good news. Someone had heard her presentation at a smaller event, appreciated her work, and recommended her to the organizers.

Her first response was excitement.

Her second was almost immediate. You are not ready for something this big.

She opened the email again. What if they realize you are not as knowledgeable as they think?

By evening, she had identified several reasons to decline. She needed more experience. She had never spoken to an audience that large. Perhaps it would be wiser to wait another year.

None of the concerns sounded irrational. That was what made them convincing.

A few days later, discussing the invitation with her older sister, she said, I just don't think I'm ready.

Her sister looked at her for a moment. You know who you sound like?

She did not.

Dad.

The answer irritated her. Their father had been dead for almost nine years.

But her sister continued. Every time you wanted to do something big, he told you not to get ahead of yourself. Remember?

She remembered. Not one conversation, but many. Be realistic. Don't embarrass yourself. There will be people there who know much more than you.

Her father had not been cruel. He had grown up in difficult circumstances and believed caution protected people from disappointment. But sitting there with her sister, she realized something she had never considered.

Her father no longer needed to tell her to be careful. She had learned to do it for him.

When Other People's Words Become Your Thoughts

We all have an internal voice. It comments on what we do, anticipates what might happen, evaluates decisions. Some of that inner conversation is useful. The problem is not that we talk to ourselves. The problem is that we often assume everything we say internally deserves to be believed simply because the voice sounds like our own.

It may not have started with us. Long before we had enough experience to form mature conclusions about ourselves, other people were giving us interpretations. Too sensitive. Not athletic. Difficult. Careless. The responsible one. Some of these descriptions may have contained truth. Others may have reflected another person's frustration, fear, or limitations.

But when a message is repeated often enough, especially by someone important to us, we may eventually stop hearing it as something they said. We begin saying it to ourselves.

Familiar Does Not Mean True

A thought you have repeated for twenty years does not arrive sounding like an opinion. It arrives sounding like knowledge. I am terrible at making decisions. I am not leadership material. The thought may feel settled because it has been present so long. But repetition proves familiarity, not accuracy. You can rehearse an incorrect conclusion for decades.

This matters especially when the conclusion was formed in childhood. Children are excellent observers and limited interpreters. A child repeatedly corrected for talking may conclude, I talk too much, when the adults around them simply preferred unusually quiet children. The child experiences the result. The child does not always have enough information to interpret the cause accurately, and the conclusion can survive into adulthood anyway.

WHOSE VOICE IS THAT?

One of the simplest questions we can ask about a recurring thought is also one of the most revealing. Who does this sound like?

You may hear your mother's anxiety in the way you imagine everything that could go wrong. Your father's criticism may appear whenever you make a mistake. A former partner's insults may still shape the way you see your appearance. Sometimes the original speaker is not one person. It may be an entire environment, a family, a school, a culture.

This book has asked a version of this question in several places by now, in a chapter about the words that first installed a belief, in a chapter about a wound and the meaning attached to it. This is where the question finally gets its full room. The point was never to blame everyone who influenced you. The point is to identify the source so you can finally evaluate the message instead of automatically repeating it.

NOT EVERY CRITICAL VOICE IS AN ENEMY

It would be easy to turn this work into a search for everyone who said something negative about us. That would miss the point. Some criticism was accurate. Growth requires the ability to receive uncomfortable truth.

Healthy correction identifies something specific. You need to prepare more carefully. You have been avoiding this responsibility. A destructive internal voice usually goes further. You are incompetent. You will never change. One addresses behavior. The other issues a verdict. Learning to question internal voices does not mean surrounding yourself with flattering thoughts. It means learning the difference between guidance and condemnation.

THE VOICE THAT PREDICTS DISASTER

Some internal voices do not criticize who we are. They constantly warn us about what might happen. Don't take the risk. Don't trust them. Don't get excited yet.

Caution has value. But there is a difference between wisdom and a mind trained to expect danger. If you grew up around instability, fear may have been presented as responsibility. Eventually caution becomes automatic. The person no longer needs anyone else to discourage them. They can produce every objection internally before hope has had enough time to form.

This voice often presents itself as maturity. I'm just being realistic. Sometimes you are. Sometimes you are repeating an old fear with adult vocabulary. The way to tell the difference is not to ignore risk. It is to examine it. What specifically could go wrong. How likely is it. Fear prefers vague catastrophe. Wisdom can usually become specific.

THE VOICE OF COMPARISON

There is another voice that rarely speaks about you without mentioning someone else. Look how far ahead they are. They have more.

Comparison creates an unusual internal standard because the target keeps changing. If your inner voice requires you to outperform other people before allowing you to feel secure, peace will remain temporary. Even winning does not solve the problem, because success simply moves you into a new group with new people to compare yourself against. Their progress is not proof of your failure. Their timing is not a judgment on yours.

WHEN YOUR OWN VOICE BECOMES CRUEL

Not every harsh internal message was directly inherited. Sometimes we become harsher with ourselves than anyone around us, replaying mistakes, insulting ourselves privately in ways we would never speak to another person.

Some people even believe harshness keeps them disciplined. If I stop criticizing myself, perhaps I will become lazy. But cruelty and accountability are not the same thing. You can acknowledge that you handled something poorly without attacking your intelligence. Ask whether the way you speak to yourself actually produces better decisions. If it produces paralysis, hiding, or endless self consciousness, it may not be discipline at all. It may simply be cruelty that has become familiar.

WHEN THE VOICE STILL HAS A PHONE NUMBER

The woman in this chapter has an advantage worth naming honestly. Her father is not calling to check whether she accepted the invitation. Not every reader has that advantage.

Sometimes the voice you are questioning belongs to someone who is still very much alive, still saying the same things, and still expecting the same response. That changes the work without canceling it. You do not need the source of a belief to update their opinion before you are allowed to update yours. You can decide that a warning no longer governs your decisions while the person who first gave it is still offering it, this Sunday, over dinner, exactly as they always have. Separating the voice from the person is, if anything, more urgent when the person is still in the room, because the two are so easy to keep confusing.

Questioning Is Not the Same as Arguing

Once people become aware of negative internal thoughts, they sometimes try to fight every one of them. This can become exhausting. You do not need to conduct a courtroom trial every time an insecure thought appears.

Sometimes it is enough to notice it. There is that thought again. I know where that came from. This creates a small but important distance between having a thought and obeying it. The goal is not a perfectly positive mind. No one has one. The goal is to become less automatic. A thought appears. You notice it. You examine whether it deserves authority. Then you decide what to do.

The Voices We Choose Matter Too

We are not only shaped by voices from the past. We are continually choosing voices in the present, in friends, mentors, podcasts, and the accounts we follow without thinking twice about it.

This works the same way, in reverse, as the curated feed this book looked at earlier, where a person's own posting quietly starts producing whatever earns the warmest response. The traffic runs the other direction here. What you keep consuming trains what starts to feel normal, true, and worth worrying about. If you spend enough time around people who constantly criticize appearance, you may begin noticing flaws you previously ignored. Healthy relationships can help correct distorted internal messages, the same way a distorted feed can quietly install new ones. What matters is whether the voices you keep choosing help you become more honest and whole, not simply more comfortable.

Developing an Inner Voice You Can Trust

Eventually the goal is not to replace one controlling voice with another. It is to develop the ability to speak to yourself with truth. That voice is neither flattering nor cruel.

You were wrong. Go make it right. You are frightened, but fear does not have enough evidence to make this decision for you. You did well. You do not need to minimize it. You need help. Ask.

This kind of inner voice does not protect us from reality. It helps us face reality without turning every difficulty into an attack on identity.

ANSWERING THE OLD VOICE DIFFERENTLY

The woman who had been invited to speak at the conference eventually accepted. Not because all her doubts disappeared. They did not.

For several weeks, the familiar warnings continued. You are not ready. But now she could hear something she had not heard before. History.

Recognizing the source did not require turning her father into a villain. She understood him better now than she had when he was alive. Caution had protected him. He had handed his children what had worked for him. She could appreciate that without carrying all of it forward.

So when the old warning appeared, she stopped trying to silence it completely. She asked questions instead. Am I actually unprepared? She knew the subject well. Are there people at the conference who know more than I do? Certainly. Did that mean she had nothing worth contributing? No.

The questions did not produce certainty. They produced proportion.

Months later, she stood backstage waiting to be introduced. Her hands were cold. The old sentence returned. Don't embarrass yourself.

For the first time, she almost smiled. She knew that voice. It had been trying to protect her for years. But protection was no longer the only thing she needed. She needed room to grow.

She walked onto the stage before the voice could finish the argument.

✦

SOUL MIRROR

Listen to the way you speak to yourself when you make a mistake or consider taking a risk. Which sentence appears most often, and if you had never heard it from anyone else, would the evidence in your life today still lead you to the same conclusion?

TIMELESS WISDOM

A thought can live inside your mind without deserving authority over your life. Maturity is not believing everything you think. It is learning which thoughts deserve to guide you, which need correcting, and which can simply be allowed to pass.

RENEWAL PRACTICE: The Six Questions

This is the fuller set promised earlier in this book. Choose one belief about yourself that has been running quietly in the background for years, and take it through all six.

Where did it originate. Who taught it to you, or what environment did.

Is it actually true, examined plainly, not simply familiar.

Does it describe something you did, or something you have decided you are.

What evidence, honestly gathered, contradicts it.

Who would you have to see differently if you stopped believing it.

What would a more accurate, more truthful voice say in its place. Not a slogan you do not believe. If the old voice says, I always fail, the accurate answer is not, I always succeed. It might be closer to, some things I attempted did not work, and failure is one possible outcome, not my identity.

Work through all six in writing, not in your head, where the old voice has home advantage. Keep the page. Its return next month does not mean you have failed to grow. It simply gives you another opportunity to decide whether a message from your past still deserves a vote in your future.

CHAPTER TWENTY-FIVE

Worth Without Performance

✦

THE FIRST THING he changed was his wardrobe.

Eighteen years at the same company had left him with a closet full of clothes that all did roughly the same job. Two weeks after the layoff, using part of the severance, he replaced most of it. New apartment next, smaller but in a better part of the city, the kind of place he had told himself for years he would move to eventually. He joined a gym for the first time since college. He rebuilt his professional profile from scratch, gave it a sharper photo and a summary that made eighteen years sound like a story he had chosen rather than a job that had ended him.

People noticed.

You look great. Honestly, this might be the best thing that could have happened to you.

He appreciated the comments because some of them were true. He was moving, trying things he had postponed for two decades, making decisions without checking them against a role that no longer existed.

But several months into the new version of his life, he began noticing something uncomfortable.

He had changed almost everything people could see. He still did not know who he was.

On quiet evenings, with nothing left to reorganize and nobody around to admire how well he was apparently doing, the same uncertainty returned. What did he actually want out of the years ahead.

Which parts of the man he had been at that company were genuinely his, and which had simply grown up around a desk he no longer sat at.

He had assumed that rebuilding his life would eventually rebuild him. He was discovering that the two were related, but not identical.

WHEN CHANGE HAPPENS ON THE OUTSIDE FIRST

External change is attractive because it is visible. You can see the new apartment, measure the weight lost, announce the new job.

These changes can be meaningful. Sometimes the environment genuinely needs to change before a person can heal. But external change has limits. You can move across the country and bring the same insecurity with you. You can lose weight and discover that the critical voice simply finds something else to criticize. You can become more successful while still needing success to reassure you that you matter.

Changing circumstances can give you a new environment. It does not automatically give you a new identity. That work happens deeper.

WHAT ARE YOU BUILDING FROM?

If you renovate a house, you eventually discover what is underneath the visible surfaces. Paint can hide cracks for a while. But if the foundation is unstable, cosmetic improvement does not solve the real problem.

Identity works similarly. You can build an impressive life on a deeply unstable belief about yourself. A person who believes they are valuable only when productive can become extraordinarily successful. The results may be admirable. The foundation may still be fragile.

This is why identity renewal cannot begin only with the question, what kind of life do I want. There is another question underneath it. What do I believe the person living that life is worth before any of it happens. If your answer depends entirely on achievement, approval, appearance, or status, the new life may eventually recreate the same old pressure in a different form. Rebuilding from the inside out means establishing something sturdier beneath what you do.

Identity Is Not a List of Compliments

When people begin working on self worth, they are sometimes encouraged to replace negative descriptions with positive ones. I am powerful. I am extraordinary.

There is nothing wrong with encouraging language. But identity cannot be rebuilt simply by exchanging insults for compliments, because some positive labels create the same problem as negative ones. They still require evidence. If I need to be successful, what happens when I fail. If I define myself as strong, what happens when I need help.

A stable identity needs room for ordinary humanity. You can be capable and confused. Strong and tired. Confident in one area and uncertain in another. Healthy identity does not require turning yourself into an impressive collection of adjectives. It requires becoming more truthful about your worth beneath all of them.

Discovering What You Actually Value

One consequence of living through borrowed identities is that we can become very clear about what is expected of us and surprisingly unclear about what actually matters to us. We know what our profession rewards, what our culture admires, what makes other people proud. But what do you value. Not what sounds admirable. What genuinely matters enough that you want your life organized around it.

Values give identity direction because they help us choose what kind of person we want to be regardless of what circumstances provide. A title can be taken away. A value can still be practiced. You can lose a position and remain honest. Experience rejection and remain compassionate. Circumstances affect what is possible. Values influence who you are while facing what is possible.

BECOMING SOMEONE YOU CAN RECOGNIZE

There is a particular exhaustion that comes from repeatedly behaving against what you know matters to you. You say yes when you want to say no. Perform confidence while privately living in fear.

Over time, the distance between your inner convictions and your outer life can become so large that you begin feeling unfamiliar to yourself. Rebuilding identity requires reducing that distance. This does not mean saying everything you think or following every feeling. But there should be enough agreement between what you believe and how you live that you can recognize yourself in your decisions. Self respect grows partly through this kind of consistency. You begin trusting yourself because your actions increasingly reflect what you say matters.

SMALL DECISIONS BUILD IDENTITY

We often imagine transformation through dramatic decisions. Sometimes those are necessary. But much of identity is rebuilt through choices too small for anyone else to notice.

You tell the truth when an excuse would be easier. You stop apologizing for a reasonable boundary. You admit you do not know something. You return to something you abandoned because you were afraid of being bad at it.

One decision rarely changes identity. Repeated decisions create evidence. Eventually you are no longer merely telling yourself you are becoming more honest, courageous, or self respecting. You have memories of behaving that way. The new identity begins acquiring history.

LEARNING TO TRUST YOURSELF AGAIN

For some people, rebuilding identity requires restoring trust in their own judgment. Perhaps you ignored warning signs, made a decision you deeply regret, stayed too long or left too quickly. After enough disappointment with our own decisions, we can become afraid of ourselves.

Advice can be valuable. But there is a difference between seeking counsel and outsourcing your life. Self trust is not the belief that you will always make the right decision. Nobody can promise that. It is the confidence that you can make a decision thoughtfully, respond honestly if you are wrong, and learn without abandoning yourself. That kind of trust grows slowly, the same way trust is rebuilt in any relationship, through consistency. The goal is not certainty. It is becoming a person whose own voice can once again be included in the room.

Stop Building for an Audience

One of the clearest signs that identity is becoming more internal is that some decisions stop needing witnesses. You begin doing things because they matter to you even when nobody will applaud.

This book already spent a full chapter on what happens when a life gets built specifically for an audience, the self constructed for a feed, edited until it says exactly what was intended. The same mechanism operates offline, more quietly. There may be no congratulations, no dramatic reveal, no one saying how much you have changed. But there is a different kind of satisfaction in becoming someone you respect when nobody is watching. An identity that requires an audience remains vulnerable to the audience. An identity built internally can appreciate recognition without depending on it.

Rebuilding Does Not Mean Starting From Nothing

When people realize that parts of their identity were built around approval, fear, or roles, they sometimes feel as though everything about them must now be questioned. That is unnecessary. You are not a demolished building site.

Perhaps pleasing people taught you attentiveness, and you can keep the attentiveness without surrendering your boundaries. Perhaps being the strong one developed resilience, and you can keep the resilience while learning to receive care. This book made a version of this same argument earlier, about keeping the wisdom a hard season taught you without keeping every defense that season required. It applies here just as directly. Renewal is not rejection of everything you became. It is discernment. What is genuinely mine. What was protection. What remains useful. What have I outgrown.

LIVING BEFORE YOU FEEL COMPLETELY READY

There is a temptation to turn identity work into another waiting room. I will speak up when I am fully confident. I will pursue the opportunity when I no longer feel afraid.

But identity often develops while we are living, not before. Confidence frequently follows action. You do not have to finish becoming before you begin living differently. There may never be a morning when every old voice disappears and you feel completely certain about who you are. Renewal is often less dramatic. You notice the old pattern. You choose differently. The pattern returns. You choose differently again. Over time, what once felt unnatural becomes familiar.

BACK IN THE APARTMENT

Nearly a year after the layoff, he stood in his new kitchen cooking dinner for a few friends.

The apartment still looked good, but he had stopped noticing the countertops months ago. What he noticed instead was something smaller. One friend mentioned a job opening at his old company's biggest competitor, practically the same role, probably the same salary, and clearly meant as good news.

He found himself pausing before answering.

I don't think that's actually what I want anymore.

The answer surprised him. Not because he had decided never to work in that field again. He might. But for once the answer wasn't coming from panic about needing a title back as fast as possible.

He had spent the last several months discovering what he actually enjoyed when there was no company expecting anything from him. He had gone back to the woodworking he'd abandoned in his twenties because it never seemed practical. He had gotten more intentional about two friendships he had let go quiet for years. He was learning which parts of his old working life he genuinely missed and which parts he had only kept because they were familiar.

Some days he still felt uncertain. But uncertainty no longer frightened him the way it had in the first months.

He had spent years assuming identity was something he should already know, a finished version of himself sitting somewhere inside, waiting to be uncovered. He understood it differently now. Part of identity is discovered. Part of it is inherited. Part of it is shaped by what happens to us. And part of it is built, deliberately, through the choices made once a person becomes conscious enough to choose.

The new apartment had changed the room. The deeper rebuilding had taken longer, and nobody could photograph most of it. There was no dramatic before and after. But he could feel the difference in ordinary decisions.

He had stopped asking only, what will make my life look complete again.

He had begun asking a better question. What kind of person do I want to be while I am living it.

That question did not hand him a finished identity. It gave him a direction.

And sometimes direction is where rebuilding actually begins.

✦

SOUL MIRROR

If you removed the identities attached to your work, relationships, achievements, and other people's opinions, what qualities would you still want to define the way you live?

TIMELESS WISDOM

A renewed identity is not built by finding better ways to impress yourself or other people. It grows when your worth becomes less dependent on what can change, and your life becomes more aligned with what you genuinely value. The outside may change first. The deepest rebuilding happens within.

RENEWAL PRACTICE: The Identity Foundation

Write five answers to this question: what do I want my life to demonstrate about the kind of person I am becoming? Avoid achievements and roles. Instead of successful, consider honest, courageous, compassionate, disciplined, or present, whichever words genuinely matter to you rather than merely sound admirable.

Take each quality and identify one small behavior that would make it visible in ordinary life. If you chose honest, perhaps there is a conversation in which you need to stop pretending everything is fine. If you chose present, perhaps someone you love needs an hour in which your attention is not divided.

Do not attempt all five at once. Choose one quality and one action. Practice it. Then practice it again.

Identity is not rebuilt in a single declaration. It becomes stronger every time the life you are living begins to agree with the person you have decided to become.

CHAPTER TWENTY-SIX

What Am I For

✦

NOTHING HAD GONE wrong.

That was the strange part. Her youngest left for college in August, exactly on schedule, exactly the way it was supposed to happen. There was no crisis behind it, no ending she hadn't seen coming for eighteen years. She still had her job, the same job she'd had for over a decade and mostly liked. Her marriage was fine, better than fine most weeks. Nothing had been taken from her.

And yet the house was quiet in a way it had never once been quiet before, and by the second week of September she found herself standing in the kitchen at four in the afternoon, the exact hour she used to start dinner for whichever child had practice that night, with absolutely nothing that needed doing.

She had expected to feel relief. Some of her friends had warned her about grief, and she had braced for that instead. What she had not expected was this other thing, something closer to a question than a feeling, arriving in the empty half hour before her husband got home.

What am I actually for now?

Not what was she for as a mother. She still was one, and would be for the rest of her life, in whatever shape that took from here. The question was stranger than that. For twenty two years, in ways she had never once had to examine, being needed by small people in a specific house had answered something underneath the surface of her days without her ever having to ask it directly.

Now the small people were not so small, and were not in the house, and the question that had been quietly answered for over two decades was simply sitting there, unanswered, in an ordinary kitchen on an ordinary Tuesday.

Identity and Purpose Are Related, but They Are Not the Same

There is a reason questions about identity eventually lead to questions about purpose.

Once you begin separating yourself from labels, roles, approval, and other people's expectations, an empty space can appear. If I am not merely what I do, then what should I do? If achievement is not the measure of my worth, why achieve anything at all?

Identity tells you something about who is living the life. Purpose asks what that life is being given to. The two belong together, but confusing them creates problems. If purpose becomes identity, losing a role can make you feel as though you have lost yourself. But if identity has no expression at all, self discovery can become strangely self absorbed, years spent examining yourself without ever asking what the healthier self is actually going to contribute.

The goal of becoming whole is not simply to become more comfortable inside yourself. It is to become freer to live well.

Purpose Is Larger Than Occupation

One of the most common mistakes people make is assuming purpose must be a role. Teacher. Executive. Parent. Those may be meaningful expressions of purpose, but they are roles, and roles can change. A teacher retires. A business closes. Children grow up and move out on a schedule everyone could see coming for years.

If purpose exists only inside a particular role, every major transition becomes an identity emergency. A deeper understanding of purpose asks what has been moving through the role. Perhaps a mother who spent two decades raising children discovers she has an unusual ability to create order out of chaos, patience out of exhaustion, calm in a room that is not calm. Parenting was one expression of that ability. It does not have to be the last one.

Sometimes we spend so much time looking for one grand purpose that we overlook the thread already running through our lives.

THE CLUES ARE OFTEN ORDINARY

Purpose is frequently discussed as though everyone should expect a dramatic moment of discovery. Some people do have one. Most lives are less theatrical.

Purpose often becomes visible through repetition. What kinds of problems do people naturally bring to you? What do you notice that other people seem to miss? What kind of work leaves you tired but satisfied rather than merely depleted? What do you enjoy making better?

These questions do not produce a magical answer. They produce clues. A person may discover that across completely different seasons of life, they have always been the one who trains new people, or the one friends come to when a decision needs clarity, or the one who notices when someone quiet in the room is struggling. Purpose is sometimes less about discovering something entirely new and more about recognizing what has quietly been present for years.

WHAT COMES NATURALLY STILL HAS VALUE

We often underestimate what comes easily to us. If you are naturally good at listening, you may assume everybody listens that way. If you naturally notice when someone is uncomfortable in a room, you may consider that ordinary.

It is ordinary to you. That does not mean it is common. One reason people miss important parts of their contribution is that they are looking for something that feels extraordinary from the inside, when abilities often feel most ordinary to the person who possesses them, simply because they have lived with them for years. This does not mean every natural ability is a life purpose. But repeated ability, genuine interest, and the needs around you can begin pointing in the same direction. Pay attention when they do.

Purpose Does Not Have to Be Impressive

The pressure to have an impressive purpose has created a new kind of anxiety. People feel they should be changing the world, reaching thousands, leaving behind a legacy strangers will discuss after they are gone.

But size and significance are not the same thing. A person can have enormous visibility and contribute very little of lasting value. Another can spend a lifetime affecting a relatively small number of people deeply. The parent who creates a healthy home after generations of chaos may never receive public recognition. The manager who treats employees with dignity may alter the course of someone's career without ever knowing it. Purpose becomes distorted when significance requires an audience. A meaningful life is not necessarily a famous one.

Purpose Changes Shape Across Seasons

What your life is for at twenty five may not look exactly the same at fifty five. This does not mean you missed your purpose earlier. Life develops.

A young adult may spend a season primarily building competence and stability. A parent with small children may have less freedom for certain ambitions because responsibility is rightly consuming significant energy. Later, the same person may have more time, wisdom, and experience to contribute differently. The deeper thread may remain while its expression changes entirely. You may always care about helping people grow, but at one stage that happens through parenting, at another through mentoring, later through something you cannot yet picture. A role ending does not necessarily mean purpose ended. Sometimes purpose is simply changing clothes.

When Pain Influences Purpose

Difficult experiences often affect what we care about. Someone who grew up without financial stability may become passionate about helping families understand money. Someone who survived a destructive relationship may later help others recognize patterns they once could not name.

This can be meaningful. But pain needs to be handled carefully when it becomes connected to purpose. You do not owe the world a career built from your wound. You are allowed to heal something without turning it into your profession. You are allowed to survive an experience without spending the rest of your life talking about it. The question is not, how can I make my pain useful so that it was worth happening. Some things were not worth happening. A better question is, now that this is part of my story, what do I want to do with the wisdom I have gained. You get to answer that.

Purpose Without Proving

There is another trap worth noticing, particularly after everything this book has already examined about performance.

Purpose can become a respectable new way to prove your worth. You stop chasing success and begin chasing impact. You stop needing applause for achievement and begin needing evidence that your life matters because you are helping people. The language changes. The pressure does not.

A healthier order is simpler. You do not contribute in order to become valuable. You contribute because you already have value and have something to give. That distinction protects purpose from becoming another performance. It also allows rest. There will be seasons when illness, grief, caregiving, or exhaustion reduces what you can offer. Your worth does not disappear during those seasons. Purpose should give life direction. It should not become another judge.

The Freedom to Want Something

Some people have spent so much of life responding to what was necessary that desire feels almost irresponsible. They know what they should do, what pays well, what their family expects. What they want is less certain.

Desire is not always trustworthy, and maturity requires discernment. But constantly distrusting desire creates another problem. You may become so responsible that you build an entire life around obligation and then wonder why you feel absent from it. Curiosity matters. Enjoyment matters. The things that make you feel awake matter, not because every enjoyable activity must become a career, but because a life constructed entirely from duty can become emotionally thin. You are allowed to ask what you want to create, learn, or explore. The answer does not have to justify itself immediately.

The Needs Around You Matter

Purpose is not discovered only by looking inward. Eventually you have to look around. What does your family need? Your community? What problem are you actually positioned to help solve?

Purpose exists where the person you are meets a world that contains needs beyond you. This protects us from making purpose entirely about personal fulfillment. Sometimes meaningful work is enjoyable. Sometimes it is inconvenient. A parent caring for a disabled child may not describe every part of caregiving as personally fulfilling. Purpose is not permanent excitement. It is meaningful direction. There will still be boring Tuesdays.

You May Already Be Living It

By October, a friend from her old parents' committee asked whether she would help a handful of teenagers in the neighborhood prepare for college applications, mostly reading essays, mostly just being available on weeknights.

She said yes mainly to fill a Thursday.

Within a few months she was meeting regularly with five or six teenagers who were, she slowly realized, not actually that different from the ones who used to fill her kitchen. She helped one boy stop apologizing for every sentence in his essay. She talked a girl through a rejection letter that had felt, for about a week, like the end of something important. She noticed, without meaning to, exactly which of them needed to be pushed and which needed to be left alone until they were ready.

One evening in November, after two hours helping a girl untangle a decision about which school to choose, she drove home with a feeling she had not expected to find again so soon.

Usefulness. But different this time.

No lunch to pack tomorrow. No permission slip to sign. Nobody in the room was hers by blood, and none of that seemed to matter nearly as much as she would have guessed.

She began thinking back over twenty two years of parenting and noticed that the moments she remembered most clearly were rarely the ones anyone would have put in a scrapbook. They were the quieter ones. Sitting with a child too anxious to sleep before a test. Helping a teenager see a friendship clearly when they couldn't see it themselves. Teaching someone how to apologize without collapsing into self punishment.

The ability had been there the whole time. Parenting had given it a place to operate. Parenting had not created it.

She had mistaken the house for the purpose. The house had gone quiet. What remained was the part that had mattered most all along.

She still missed the noise some evenings. But the question that had stopped her cold in the kitchen that September afternoon no longer felt quite so unanswerable.

What am I for?

She no longer needed one grand sentence. She was good at helping someone find their footing right before they needed it most. She had two decades of practice. There were people, right now, who could use exactly that.

For this season, that was enough.

✦

SOUL MIRROR

Look across your life rather than only at your current role. What kind of contribution keeps appearing, in different forms, across completely different seasons?

TIMELESS WISDOM

Purpose is not proof that your life matters. Your life matters before you accomplish anything with it. Purpose is what becomes possible once you stop spending all your energy proving your worth and start asking what you can meaningfully do with the life you already have.

RENEWAL PRACTICE: Follow the Thread

Draw a line down the center of a page. On one side, write five moments in your life when you felt genuinely useful or deeply satisfied by something you contributed, from work, family, friendship, or ordinary life. On the other side, write what you were actually doing underneath the activity. Teaching. Solving. Listening. Creating. Protecting.

Look for repetition. Then complete three sentences. I seem to come alive when I am. People often trust me to. Something I care enough about to contribute toward is.

Do not force these answers into a plan. For now, simply notice the thread, and choose one small way to express it in your present life. Purpose does not always begin with a major decision. Sometimes it begins when you recognize what has been quietly moving through your life for years, and finally give it somewhere intentional to go.

CHAPTER TWENTY-SEVEN

Learning to Belong to Yourself

✦

FOR YEARS, SHE had a habit of checking the room before checking herself.

If she told a story at dinner, she watched people's faces to see whether it was landing well. If she bought something she loved, she felt better about the purchase after someone complimented it. If she expressed an opinion and the room became quiet, she immediately began reconsidering whether she should have said anything.

She did not think of herself as insecure. In many areas she was genuinely confident. She had built a good career, raised children, handled money responsibly. But emotionally there was still a small committee living inside her head. What will they think. Am I being difficult. Should I explain myself.

Then, one evening, a friend asked her a question she could not answer.

They had been discussing a decision she was trying to make about whether to remain involved in an organization that had consumed more of her time than she wanted to give. She explained what everyone else thought. Her husband believed she should stay. Several people depended on her. She had made commitments.

Her friend listened for a while and finally asked, what do you want?

She began answering with another explanation.

No. I heard all of that, her friend said. What do you want?

She sat quietly. It was astonishing how difficult the question felt.

When You Know Everyone Except Yourself

Some people become exceptionally skilled at reading others. They know when someone is uncomfortable, sense disappointment before it is expressed, anticipate what will make a situation easier. This sensitivity can be a genuine strength.

But there is a cost when awareness of everyone else grows stronger than awareness of yourself. You know what your family needs but struggle to name what you need. This doesn't happen because you have no self. It happens because consulting yourself quietly stopped being part of the decision, so gradually that you never noticed the step going missing. You became so practiced at adjusting that adjustment began to feel like personality.

This book has already looked at several versions of this, borrowed preferences inside a close relationship, a self that disappears specifically to remain accepted somewhere. What this chapter is after is narrower and more internal than either of those. Not whether you can belong somewhere without losing yourself. Whether you can belong to yourself at all, in a room by yourself, with no one there to check.

You Are Allowed to Have Preferences

This sounds almost embarrassingly simple. You are allowed to prefer things. A restaurant. A pace of life. A way of spending your weekend.

People who have spent years adapting can become uncomfortable with this. They may answer almost every question with, I don't mind, whatever everyone wants, I'm fine with anything. Sometimes that is genuine flexibility. Sometimes it is the habit of removing yourself before anyone can disagree with you.

Learning to belong to yourself begins in surprisingly ordinary places. What do I actually like. What leaves me drained. What do I no longer want simply because I wanted it ten years ago. You do not have to turn every preference into a principle. You are simply allowed to know that you have one.

DISAPPOINTING SOMEONE DOES NOT ALWAYS MEAN YOU DID SOMETHING WRONG

For people accustomed to measuring themselves through other people's reactions, disappointment can feel like evidence of wrongdoing. Someone is unhappy with your decision, and immediately you begin examining yourself. Was I selfish. Should I reconsider.

Those are responsible questions. But another person's disappointment does not automatically answer them. Sometimes people are disappointed because you genuinely behaved badly. Sometimes they are disappointed because what you chose is simply inconvenient for them. Those are not the same thing, and confusing them is where approval quietly takes over from conscience. You can care about someone's feelings without letting their feelings become the final moral judgment on your decision. Goodness and agreeableness were never actually the same word.

BELONGING TO YOURSELF IS NOT SELFISHNESS

Near the start of this book, a promise was made that this work would not turn you inward at everyone else's expense. It is worth returning to now, because this is the chapter where the promise gets tested.

There is a version of self focus that becomes genuinely selfish, a person so preoccupied with personal needs and personal boundaries that everyone else becomes secondary. That is not what belonging to yourself means. Healthy identity does not make you less capable of relationship. It should make you better at it. When you belong to yourself, you can give without secretly requiring the gift to purchase love. You can hear another person's opinion without automatically surrendering your own. You can love someone deeply without requiring them to become the source of your worth. The goal was never independence from everyone. It is relationship without self abandonment, which is a considerably more mature form of belonging than either total accommodation or total withdrawal.

THE LONELINESS BETWEEN OLD AND NEW

There can be a genuinely lonely period during identity renewal. The old version of you no longer fits comfortably. The new version is not yet familiar. Old habits still appear. New boundaries feel awkward, and you may even wonder whether life was easier before you began examining any of this.

In some ways it probably was. Automatic living requires fewer decisions. If you always say yes, you never have to decide when to say no. If you always let other people define what is reasonable, you never have to tolerate the discomfort of disagreement. Freedom creates responsibility. Once you begin belonging to yourself, you become more responsible for the life you choose, and that can feel frightening for a while before it feels like anything else. It is also where adulthood becomes more fully your own.

BECOMING YOUR OWN SAFE PLACE

There is a kind of inner security that develops when you stop abandoning yourself the moment life becomes uncomfortable.

You make a mistake and remain on your own side while still taking responsibility for it. Someone rejects you and you grieve without immediately asking what defect the rejection must have exposed. You enter a room where you are not the most impressive person present and remain entirely comfortable occupying your chair. You receive criticism and actually examine it, rather than either swallowing it whole or throwing it out untouched. You feel afraid and do not shame yourself for being afraid. You need help and ask for it without deciding that needing help makes you weak.

This is what it means, in part, to become safe for yourself. Not to protect yourself from every uncomfortable truth. Not to excuse every mistake. But to know that whatever happens, you will not immediately join whatever is attacking you. You will listen. You will tell yourself the truth. You will correct what needs correcting, grieve what needs grieving. And you will remain, on your own side, the whole way through.

BACK AT THE TABLE

The woman eventually left the organization.

It took her three months to decide, not because the decision itself required three months, but because she kept hoping to find a version of it that disappointed nobody. There wasn't one.

When she finally told the leadership, they were disappointed. One person questioned her timing. Another reminded her how difficult she would be to replace. For several days afterward she felt terrible, and the old committee reconvened immediately. Maybe you were selfish. Maybe you should go back.

Then she did something unfamiliar. She waited. She did not reverse the decision simply to make the discomfort stop. She allowed other people to have their feelings, and she allowed herself to have hers.

A few weeks later she noticed the guilt had gone quieter. She had more time. She slept better. She began using one evening each week for something she had wanted to pursue for years. Nothing dramatic happened. Nobody congratulated her for finally choosing herself. The world simply adjusted, which turned out to be the most surprising part of all of it. For years she had imagined that disappointing people would produce consequences far larger than it usually did. People adapted. Some understood eventually. Some never completely agreed. Life continued regardless.

One evening, the same friend who had asked what she wanted called her.

How are you feeling about leaving now?

She thought before answering. I still think about whether everyone is okay without me.

Her friend laughed. Of course you do.

She laughed too. Then she added something she would not have known how to say a year earlier.

But I don't think their being okay is the only way I get to be okay anymore.

There it was. Not rebellion. Not selfishness. Not indifference. Something quieter. She had spent years trying to secure belonging by making herself easy for other people to keep. Now she was learning a different kind of belonging entirely. She could love people without living inside their expectations. She could hear their opinions without losing her own. And when a room did not approve of her, she no longer had to leave herself in order to remain inside it.

She was beginning, finally, to belong to herself.

✦

SOUL MIRROR

If nobody needed to agree with you, what would you know about your own life that you are currently afraid to admit?

TIMELESS WISDOM

Belonging to yourself does not mean needing nobody. It means you no longer have to disappear in order to remain connected. You can love deeply, listen carefully, compromise generously, and still remain present inside your own life.

RENEWAL PRACTICE: The Self Consultation

For the next seven days, notice one decision each day in which you would normally check someone else's preference before recognizing your own. Before asking anyone else, pause and answer four questions. What do I think. What do I want. What do I need. What do I believe is wise.

Then seek other people's input if the decision genuinely requires it. The purpose is not to make every choice alone. It is to make sure you are present in the conversation before anyone else joins it.

At the end of the week, look back at your answers. Notice where your own voice was easy to hear, and where it disappeared. Notice whose disappointment you were most afraid of, and whether there are places where you have quietly confused being loved with being agreeable.

Choose one small area to practice remaining present in. Express a preference without apologizing for having one. Say no without writing an essay to justify it. Allow someone to disagree without immediately changing your mind.

A self that has been abandoned repeatedly is usually rebuilt the same way, through small acts of return rather than one dramatic one. Each time you listen to yourself without becoming ruled by yourself, and each time you let someone be disappointed without making their disappointment your identity, you are practicing something deeper than confidence. You are learning how to stay with yourself. After a lifetime of looking outside yourself for permission to belong, staying may be one of the most important things left to learn.

CHAPTER TWENTY-EIGHT

The Secure Self

✦

SHE ALMOST DID not recognize the change because nothing dramatic had happened.

There had been no single breakthrough. No morning when she woke completely confident. No conversation after which every old insecurity disappeared. Life had simply continued. There were still difficult days. She still occasionally compared herself with other women. Criticism could still sting.

But something was different.

She noticed it one afternoon at a family gathering. Someone made a comment about a decision she had recently made. It was not particularly cruel, but there was enough judgment in the tone that the old version of her would have spent the rest of the evening explaining herself.

This time she listened. She considered whether there was anything useful in what had been said.

There wasn't. So she smiled and changed the subject.

That was all.

Driving home later, she realized she had not replayed the conversation. She had not constructed a better response in her head. She had not called anyone to ask whether they thought the person was right. The comment had entered her life and left again without becoming a crisis.

Perhaps this was what change looked like once it had finally become ordinary.

Security Is Quieter Than You Think

We often imagine a secure person as someone who enters every room with complete confidence, who never questions themselves, never feels intimidated, never needs reassurance. That person does not exist.

Security is not the absence of uncomfortable emotion. It is the ability to experience uncomfortable emotion without immediately losing your sense of self. A secure person can feel nervous without concluding that nervousness means they are incapable. They can be rejected and hurt without the rejection automatically becoming proof they are unworthy. They can fail and examine what went wrong without turning the failure into their name. They can succeed and enjoy it without requiring the success to establish their value.

The secure self still feels. It simply does not turn every feeling into an identity.

You No Longer Need Every Mirror

Throughout this book we have returned repeatedly to the mirrors through which people learn to see themselves. Parents, partners, culture, achievement, appearance, wounds, other people's expectations.

These mirrors matter because human beings do not develop in isolation. Security does not require breaking every mirror. It requires knowing that no single mirror contains the whole truth about you. Someone may dislike you. That is information about a relationship, not a final statement about your worth. Your career may flourish, and you can be grateful. It may struggle, and you can learn what needs learning. Neither season deserves ownership of the self. The secure person can look into mirrors without needing to live inside them.

YOU BECOME EASIER TO CORRECT

One of the surprising results of stronger identity is that correction becomes less threatening.

When identity is fragile, criticism can feel enormous. If someone tells you that you handled something badly, you may hear, you are a bad person. So you defend, explain, or collapse. But when your worth is no longer on trial in every conversation, you can become genuinely curious instead. Is there truth in this. What am I missing. Security does not make a person convinced they are always right. It gives them enough internal stability to discover when they are wrong, without needing to protect a perfect image, because they no longer need perfection to remain worthy of respect.

YOU BECOME EASIER TO CELEBRATE

Security also changes the way you respond to other people's success. When another person's beauty is not evidence against yours, you can appreciate it. When someone else's promotion does not diminish your progress, you can congratulate them sincerely.

Envy may still appear occasionally. Security does not make you superhuman. But you become better at recognizing what envy is trying to tell you, a desire, an old comparison still running, an insecurity worth understanding rather than hiding from. There is enough room in the world for another person to shine without requiring you to become dimmer.

YOU STOP NEEDING TO WIN EVERY ROOM

A secure self does not require universal approval. This does not mean becoming careless about how you affect people. Reputation matters. Character matters. But there is a difference between caring about your reputation and needing everyone to approve of you.

Some people will misunderstand you. Some will prefer the person you used to be. You cannot build a stable identity on controlling all of these reactions. At some point, maturity requires accepting that you will not win every room. You can leave some conversations without being understood and still know that you acted with integrity, even when the outcome produced no applause at all. There is enormous peace in no longer needing to manage yourself inside everybody else's mind.

YOU CAN BE BOTH STRONG AND NEEDY

Insecure identity often creates false extremes. Either I am strong or I am weak. Whole or broken. But human beings are rarely that simple.

You can be strong and need help. Confident and still want reassurance. Emotionally healthy and have a genuinely difficult week. Security allows complexity. You no longer have to defend an image of yourself as permanently strong. You can say, I don't know, I need help, that hurt me, I changed my mind, and none of those sentences threaten a secure identity, because security was never built on appearing invulnerable in the first place. Sometimes the strongest thing about a person is that they no longer need to look strong all the time.

YOU STOP TREATING GROWTH AS AN EMERGENCY

If you believe you must become completely improved before you can feel at peace with yourself, personal growth becomes a lifelong emergency. There is always another problem, another version of yourself waiting somewhere ahead.

Security changes the tone of growth. You can notice something that needs work without panicking about what its existence means. You can say, I need to become better at this, without hearing, I am not enough. Shame can produce change. Fear can produce change. But both usually demand payment later. Growth rooted in truth is slower sometimes, but it holds. You are not repairing a worthless person. You are developing a valuable one.

THE SECURE SELF HAS BOUNDARIES WITHOUT WALLS

When people have been hurt, boundaries can initially feel like protection, and sometimes protection is exactly what is needed. But security eventually asks something more. Can you protect yourself without closing yourself.

A wall says nobody gets close enough to hurt me again. A boundary says closeness requires respect. A wall assumes danger everywhere. A boundary pays attention to where danger actually is. The secure self does not trust everyone, that would not be wisdom, but neither does it assume that everyone must pay for what someone else did. You learn to watch behavior, to take your discomfort seriously, and still, when trust has genuinely been earned, to open. Security is not isolation. It is the ability to remain yourself while connected to someone else.

YOU CAN CHANGE WITHOUT BECOMING LOST

One of the fears underneath identity crisis is the fear that change will erase us. If I am no longer who I used to be, who am I.

But a secure identity has room to evolve. Your interests can change. Your priorities can shift. Changing your mind does not necessarily mean you were fake before. Sometimes it means you learned. Outgrowing a role does not mean the years you spent in it were wasted. Sometimes a season simply completed its work. There is a difference between being unstable and being alive. Living things grow.

THE SECURE SELF STILL HAS BAD DAYS

You will have days when old patterns return. Someone will say something that finds an old wound with surprising accuracy, and you will compare, overexplain, say yes when you meant no.

Do not turn recurrence into failure. Growth is not proven by never experiencing an old pattern again. Sometimes it is measured by how quickly you recognize it. What once controlled you for three years may now control you for three days. Then three hours. Eventually perhaps three minutes. That is still growth. You notice sooner. You recover faster. You return to yourself more easily. The goal was never to become a person who could no longer be shaken. The goal was to become a person who knows how to come home.

THE TOWEL

There is an old story worth telling here, near the end of this book, because it says in a single image everything the last twenty seven chapters have been trying to say in sentences.

A man sat down to dinner one evening with a group of people who had known him for years. By every account of that night, he was entirely secure in who he was, certain of where he had come from and certain of exactly where the evening, and the days after it, were taking him. And knowing that, with nothing left to prove and no reputation left to protect, he got up in the middle of the meal, tied a towel around his waist, and knelt down to wash the feet of everyone at the table, the job that belonged, in that time, to the lowest servant in the house.

Nobody at that table expected it. It is worth sitting with why he was able to do it at all. Not because he had nothing. Because he no longer needed that particular room to see him a particular way. A person still auditioning for a room does not kneel down in the middle of dinner and pick up a towel. Only someone who already knows exactly who they are has that kind of freedom left over to spend on somebody else.

Worth precedes performance. That has been the order underneath this entire book, stated a dozen different ways in a dozen different chapters. You do not work in order to become worthy. You work from worth already given, before the title, before the money, before anyone applauded, before you had accomplished anything that could be placed on a résumé. There was already something valuable there. This does not make achievement meaningless. It puts achievement in its proper place, expression rather than proof, the towel rather than the argument for why you deserved to be at the table in the first place.

COMING HOME TO YOURSELF

Several years after that family gathering, the woman found herself in another room where she did not quite fit.

The conversation turned toward careers, accomplishments, what everyone's children were doing. There had been a time when a gathering like this would have activated an internal accounting system. Who had more. Was she impressive enough.

This time she noticed the old instinct beginning. Then something else happened. She became interested in the people instead. She asked questions. She listened to someone describe a project she knew almost nothing about, and meant her compliment when she gave it.

At one point someone mentioned an accomplishment far beyond anything she had achieved in that area. She felt the brief sting of comparison. Then it passed. Not because she had convinced herself she was better. Not because she had reminded herself of everything she had accomplished. She simply did not need the comparison to finish.

That surprised her. Years earlier, she had believed confidence meant finally gathering enough evidence to prove she was equal to everyone around her. Now she understood that freedom was not needing to calculate equality at all. She did not need to be the most impressive person in the room, and she did not need to become smaller because somebody else was. She could simply occupy her own life.

On the drive home, she thought about how much energy she had once spent trying to answer one question. Am I enough? It occurred to her that she no longer asked it very often. Not because every insecurity had been resolved. Not because life had finally handed her enough evidence. Perhaps she had simply stopped believing the question needed answering every single day.

She was still becoming. Still learning. Still occasionally wrong. Still capable of being hurt, and still capable of hurting others and needing to repair what she had done. Still human.

But she was no longer waiting for some final version of herself to arrive before she could belong inside her own life. She had stopped auditioning for herself.

And perhaps that is what security finally becomes. Not a life without questions. Not confidence without interruption. But a quiet place inside from which you can meet success without worshipping it, failure without becoming it, love without disappearing into it, criticism without collapsing beneath it, and change without losing yourself.

The world will continue offering mirrors. Some will show you something useful. Some will distort you. You can look. You can learn. You can adjust. But you no longer have to ask every mirror who you are.

You know enough now to come home.

✦

SOUL MIRROR

At the beginning of this book, you may have asked some version of the question, who am I really. Ask it again now, but this time do not answer first with your work, your relationships, your wounds, or what other people call you. What remains?

TIMELESS WISDOM

Security is not finally becoming impressive enough that nobody can question your worth. It is becoming rooted deeply enough that your worth is no longer renegotiated every time life changes. You can grow without rejecting yourself, change without losing yourself, and be misunderstood without disappearing. Your life does not need to become perfect for you to become whole.

FINAL RENEWAL PRACTICE: The Identity Declaration

Find somewhere quiet. Take a fresh page. Do not begin by writing who you want to become. Begin with what you are ready to stop using as evidence about your worth.

Complete these sentences.

I am no longer willing to define myself primarily by. Write whatever belongs there, a failure, a relationship, a wound, an old family role, an achievement, another person's opinion.

I can acknowledge that ______ is part of my story without allowing it to become the whole story.

The qualities I want to live from are. Choose a small number. Not impressive words. True ones.

When I forget who I am, I want to remember.

Finally, write this line and mean it as fully as you can: the life I am building from here will not be an attempt to prove that I matter. It will be an expression of the truth that I already do.

Read the page slowly. This is not a magical declaration that erases years of experience. It is a marker, a decision about the direction you intend to keep walking. Keep it somewhere you can return to, because there will be seasons when an old mirror becomes convincing again.

When that happens, return. Not to a perfect version of yourself, and not to the person you were before life became complicated. Return to the deeper truth you have been uncovering across these pages.

You are more than what happened to you. More than what you accomplished. More than who stayed, and more than who left. More than the roles you performed, and more than the version of yourself you built simply to survive.

You are still here.

And now, perhaps, you can begin living from the inside out. Not trying to become worthy of your own life.

Finally learning how to inhabit it.

CONCLUSION

You Were Never Only One Thing

✦

PERHAPS YOU BEGAN this book because something about yourself had become difficult to understand.

Maybe you had reached a season when the roles that once gave your life definition were changing. Perhaps a relationship ended, a career shifted, children grew up, success did not satisfy you the way you expected, or failure affected you more deeply than you thought it would.

Perhaps nothing dramatic happened at all. You simply became tired of living according to versions of yourself that no longer felt completely true.

The strong one. The successful one. The one everybody depends on. The overlooked one. The wounded one. The person who always has everything together.

Some of those descriptions may contain truth. None of them contain all of you. That has been one of the central discoveries of this journey. You were never only one thing.

The Person Beneath the Names

Long before you knew how to explain yourself, people were helping you form an identity. Some did it intentionally. Others had no idea they were doing it. A parent's words mattered. What your culture celebrated mattered. Who stayed and who left mattered.

Over time, these experiences accumulated. Some became memories. Some became beliefs. Some became voices you still hear. And eventually you may have stopped noticing the difference between who you were and what life had taught you to become.

That does not mean everything you learned was wrong. Your history gave you real strengths, discipline, compassion, perseverance, capacities you would never willingly have chosen to learn the hard way. The purpose of renewal was never to look backward and reject everything that formed you. It was to look honestly. To keep what is true. To release what became harmful. And to stop confusing what happened along the way with the full definition of the person who traveled through it.

YOU DO NOT HAVE TO HATE WHO YOU WERE

There may be parts of your former self you now understand differently. How desperately you wanted approval. How often you said yes when you meant no. How hard you worked to look strong.

It is tempting, once these patterns become clear, to become embarrassed by the person who lived them. Try not to. That person was working with what they knew. Some of your patterns were attempts to find love. Some were attempts to stay safe. You can outgrow a version of yourself without despising the person who needed to become that version.

Renewal is not an argument with your past. It is a more truthful relationship with it. I understand why I became that person. I understand what that version of me was trying to protect. I no longer need to live exactly that way. There is real maturity in holding gratitude and release in the same hand.

HEALING DOES NOT ERASE HISTORY

You will still remember. The things that happened do not disappear because you understand them better. There may still be names that bring back emotion, comments that occasionally find an old insecurity.

Healing does not require amnesia. It changes your relationship with memory. You can remember rejection without reliving your worthlessness. You can remember what you lost and still recognize what remains. A healed memory is not necessarily a painless one. Sometimes it is simply a memory that no longer gets to make today's decisions.

YOU WILL STILL NEED OTHER PEOPLE

Becoming secure does not mean becoming self contained. You will still need encouragement, correction, love, wisdom. There will be seasons when another person's voice helps you remember something you have temporarily forgotten about yourself. That is not weakness.

The goal was never to become so independent that nobody could affect you. It was to become secure enough that relationship no longer requires self erasure. You can receive love without making another person responsible for your worth. You can belong deeply to other people while still belonging to yourself. That is not isolation. It is healthier connection.

THERE IS NO FINAL VERSION OF YOU

Perhaps one of the greatest pressures we place on ourselves is the idea that somewhere ahead there is a finished person. Completely confident. Never triggered. Never afraid.

You do not need to become that person. You could spend the rest of your life chasing them and miss the life you are actually living. You will continue changing, the way everything alive continues changing. There will be future versions of you that you cannot imagine from where you are standing today. Let them come. A secure identity does not require remaining exactly the same. It gives you somewhere stable enough from which to change.

When You Forget

And you will forget. There will be a room where you suddenly feel inadequate again, a moment when an old voice sounds convincing.

When that happens, do not panic. Do not decide that none of this worked. Notice what is happening. Ask what has been touched. Separate the event from the meaning you are giving it. Then return.

You are not the room's opinion of you. You are not your worst decision. You are not the title on your door, or the number in your account, or the body you had at twenty five. You are not even the wound that changed you. All of these things may belong somewhere in your story. They do not get to become the author.

A Life Lived From the Inside Out

Underneath this entire journey has sat one quiet claim, easy to state and hard to actually live inside: your life has value before the world decides what to call it. Before achievement, there is worth. Before anyone chooses you, there is worth. And when failure eventually arrives, that worth does not disappear along with it.

This changes the direction from which life gets lived. Instead of spending your years asking the world to confirm that you matter, you begin living as someone whose life already does. You can still build, achieve, lead, love, become excellent at what you do. There is no need to become smaller in order to become secure. The difference is that none of it carries the impossible weight of making you worthy anymore. It becomes an expression of a life rather than evidence for its value.

You are free to succeed because success no longer has to save you. Free to fail because failure no longer has permission to name you. Free to love because someone else's love is no longer your only proof that you are lovable. This is what renewal makes possible. Not a smaller life. A freer one.

ELEVEN MONTHS LATER

She had said, that afternoon in the hospital gown, that she would think about the chaplain's question. And she had, on and off, for eleven months, the way a person thinks about something without quite deciding to do anything about it yet.

What finally moved her was smaller than she expected. An ordinary Tuesday evening, nothing scheduled, and she found a pen and a blank page and did something that felt, at the time, faintly ridiculous. She wrote twenty sentences beginning with the words I am, and then went back through and crossed out every one that named a job, a relationship, or something she did for somebody else.

Two sentences survived.

She sat with that for a long time.

It did not fix anything that evening. She did not walk away with a tidy answer to who she was, and this book was never going to hand her one either. But something had shifted, quietly, the same way most of what matters in a life tends to shift, not in the hospital room where the question was first asked, but on an unremarkable Tuesday, months later, with a pen and two surviving sentences and a willingness to keep going from there.

If you met her now, she would still tell you she works in accounting, that she is a mother, that people at the office call her reliable. All of that would still be true. But it would no longer be the whole of what she offered you if you asked her, genuinely, who she was. She has other sentences now. Fewer of them than she expected, and more of them than she had that afternoon with the chaplain, and she is still adding to the list, slowly, the way anyone does.

The question that stopped her cold in that hospital room has not disappeared. It simply is not the only question left standing anymore.

THE NEXT QUESTION

We began with a question. Who am I?

You are a person with history, but you are more than your history. You have roles, but you are more than your roles. You have wounds, but you are more than what wounded you.

So perhaps the question at the end of this book is slightly different from the one it opened with. Not only, who am I. But, now that I am beginning to understand who I am, how do I want to live?

That question takes identity out of the mirror and places it into an actual life. How will you speak to yourself. What will you stop tolerating. What will you pursue now that you no longer need the pursuit to prove your worth. What old voice will no longer receive the final word.

You do not have to answer everything today. This was never about producing a perfect definition of yourself. It was about becoming free enough to stop living inside definitions that were too small.

So continue. Live. Build. Rest. Risk. Make mistakes, and repair them. Let people know you, and let some people misunderstand you anyway. Celebrate what you accomplish. Grieve what you lose. And through all of it, remember that circumstances will keep changing around you. You do not have to start yourself over every time they do.

You were never only the successful self, or the wounded self, or the invisible self, or any of the other selves you met in these pages. They were windows. Not the whole house. You are larger than any single chapter of your life, including this one.

Perhaps the work ahead is not to spend another lifetime searching for yourself. Perhaps it is to take the self you are finally learning to know, and give that person permission to live.

Not someday. Not when everyone understands. Not when every wound has disappeared.

Now.

Your identity does not need to become a finished product. It needs to become a place from which you can live.

And from here, you can.

About the Author

Dr. Toyin Ogundipe

✦

Dr. Toyin Ogundipe is an author, teacher, consultant, mentor, and transformational leader whose work centers on a deeply human question: What does it take for a person to become whole from the inside out?

Across her years of teaching, leadership, mentoring, professional practice, and service to others, she has encountered people from remarkably different backgrounds who often carry remarkably similar struggles. They may be accomplished yet uncertain of their worth. Strong for everyone else yet privately exhausted. Successful in public while carrying wounds that have never been given language. Some have spent years living according to expectations placed upon them by family, culture, relationships, success, failure, or painful experiences, without ever stopping long enough to ask who they truly are beneath it all.

These encounters have helped shape Dr. Ogundipe's conviction that many of the struggles visible in a person's life have deeper roots within the soul: in what people believe about themselves, the meaning they have given their experiences, the words they have internalized, the relationships that formed them, and the wounds they learned to carry.

Her writing is therefore concerned not merely with helping people feel better, but with helping them understand themselves more truthfully.

Dr. Ogundipe brings together timeless wisdom, practical insight, an understanding of human behavior, and principles rooted in the biblical view of human worth and wholeness. Rather than presenting these ideas primarily through religious language, she translates them into the ordinary experiences of life: identity, fear, anxiety, relationships, emotional dependence, rejection, forgiveness, resentment, trauma, healing, purpose, and the difficult work of learning to live freely after being hurt.

Her approach is intentionally accessible.

She believes profound truth does not need complicated language to be powerful. The person who has spent years struggling with insecurity should not need an advanced degree to understand why. The person recovering from emotional pain should be able to recognize their own life in the pages they are reading. And the person who has achieved outward success while remaining unsettled within should encounter language that helps explain what accomplishment alone could never repair.

This conviction became part of the foundation for The Soul Renewal Series, a seven-book journey created to help readers examine the inner patterns that shape their lives and move toward greater emotional freedom, stability, self-understanding, and wholeness.

The Identity Crisis, the first book in the series, begins at the foundation: the self.

It explores the identities we inherit, perform, protect, and sometimes lose ourselves trying to maintain. It invites readers to examine the voices, experiences, relationships, achievements, wounds, and expectations that have participated in answering the question, Who am I? It then helps them begin separating what happened to them from who they fundamentally are.

For Dr. Ogundipe, however, writing about renewal is not simply an intellectual exercise.

It grows from a larger life commitment to helping people become whole.

She has spent significant portions of her life teaching, mentoring, developing leaders, serving communities, and investing in people, often in environments where transformation matters more than recognition. Her work reflects a belief that knowledge reaches its highest value when it helps another human being live differently.

At the foundation of her worldview is the conviction that every human life possesses inherent worth and that people are capable of growth, restoration, and meaningful change. Her Christian faith informs this understanding deeply, while her writing in The Soul Renewal Series is intentionally welcoming to readers from a wide range of backgrounds who are searching for wisdom, healing, clarity, and a healthier relationship with themselves.

Dr. Ogundipe does not write from the assumption that healthy people never struggle.

She writes from the understanding that wholeness is not perfection.

It is learning to recognize what has shaped you without allowing everything that shaped you to continue defining you. It is developing enough inner stability to face truth without shame, experience love without losing yourself, pursue success without making achievement your identity, and move through life's inevitable changes without continually forgetting your worth.

Through her writing and speaking, Dr. Toyin Ogundipe continues to pursue the mission at the heart of her work:

✦

Helping people become whole in spirit, soul, and life, through timeless wisdom that transforms from the inside out.